W9-BNQ-400

Welcome to Encyclopædia Britannica's *Space*. This book introduces you to major historical developments in space exploration, offers a close-up view of the planets, and concludes with a look at the fascinating objects that lie beyond our solar system.

The SD-X Reader lets you get the most out of your book. With the SD-X Reader, you can access hours of audio content with a touch of the Reader to the page. More than 700 audio touchpoints in this book let you hear key vocabulary, learn in-depth information, and engage in interactive activities and learning games.

Reinforce learning with fun interactive games.

- **Look and Find**
- **True or False**
- **Multiple Choice and more**

Touch pictures, words, or buttons to play.

A touch of the Reader lets you hear definitions and pronunciations for key vocabulary.

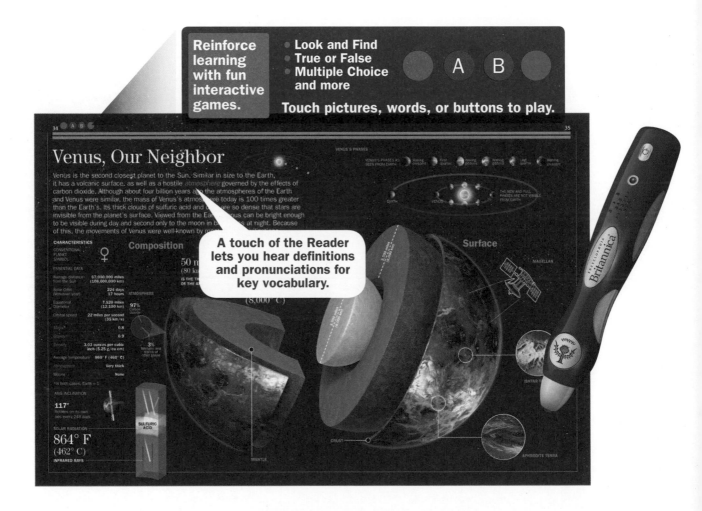

To order the SD-X Reader, go to **PILInteractive.com**, where you can also order additional books in the Encyclopædia Britannica Science Library.

The SD-X Reader can be used for all six books in the Encyclopædia Britannica Science Library.

Britannica
Animals
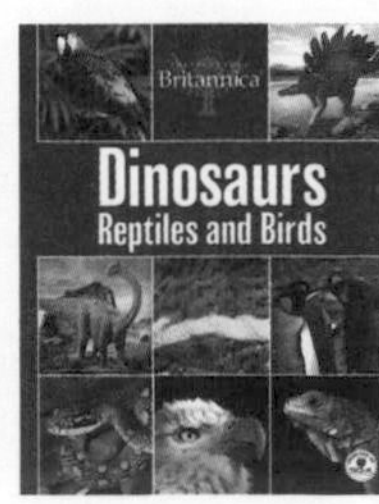
Britannica
Dinosaurs
Reptiles and Birds

Britannica
Earth
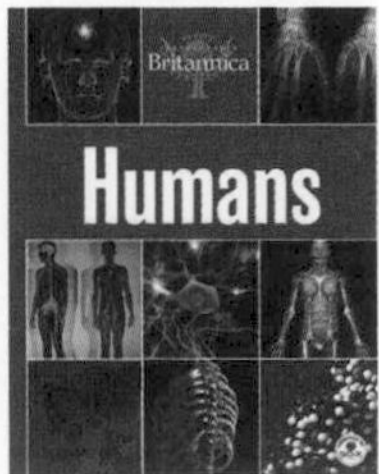
Britannica
Humans

Britannica
Space
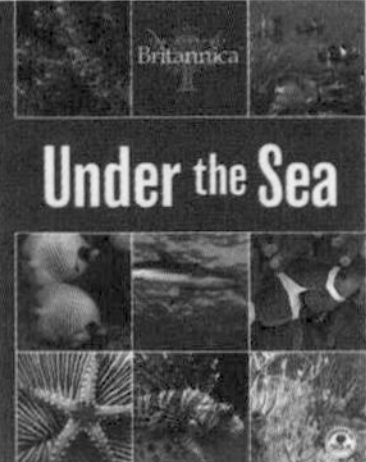
Britannica
Under the Sea

SPACE

How to Use Your SD-X Reader with This Book

This highly informative book introduces you and your child to outer space in a new interactive format. You can read the book and study the rich illustrations, but a touch of the SD-X Reader adds in-depth audio information, word definitions, and learning games to the pictures and text.

1. Press the Power button to turn the SD-X Reader on or off. The LED will light up when the SD-X Reader is on.

2. Touch the volume buttons found on this page or on the Table of Contents page in this book to adjust the volume.

3. Throughout the book, words in this color provide additional information when they're touched with the SD-X Reader. Objects on the page may also play additional audio.

4. At the top left corner of each spread, you'll see circles like these: Touch a circle to start a learning game or quiz. Touch the same circle again to stop playing the game. Touch another circle to start another learning game or quiz.

5. Some learning games will ask you to use T F buttons or A B buttons to answer. For other learning games, touch objects on the page to answer.

6. When you've answered all the questions in a learning game, you'll hear your score.

7. After two minutes of inactivity, the SD-X Reader will beep and go to sleep.

8. If the batteries are low, the SD-X Reader will beep twice and the LED will start blinking. Replace the batteries by following the instructions on the next page. The SD-X Reader uses two AAA batteries.

9. To use headphones or earbuds, plug them into the headphone jack on the bottom of the SD-X Reader.

CHANGE THE VOLUME WITH THESE BUTTONS:

UP DOWN

Battery Information
Includes two replaceable AAA batteries (UM-4 or LR03).

Battery Installation
1. Open battery door with small screwdriver.
2. Install new batteries according to +/- polarity. If batteries are not installed properly, the device will not function.
3. Replace battery door; secure with small screw.

Battery Safety
Batteries must be replaced by adults only. Properly dispose of used batteries. See battery manufacturer for disposal recommendations. Do not mix alkaline, standard (carbon-zinc), or rechargeable (nickel-cadmium) batteries. Do not mix old and new batteries. Only recommended batteries of the same or equivalent type should be used. Remove weakened or dead batteries. Never short-circuit the supply terminals. Non-rechargeable batteries are not to be recharged. Do not use rechargeable batteries. If batteries are swallowed, in the USA, promptly see a doctor and have the doctor phone 1-202-625-3333 collect. In other countries, have the doctor call your local poison control center. This product uses 2 AAA batteries (2 X 1.5V = 3.0 V). Use batteries of the same or equivalent type as recommended. The supply terminals are not to be short-circuited. Batteries should be changed when sounds mix, distort, or become otherwise unintelligible as batteries weaken. The electrostatic discharge may interfere with the sound module. If this occurs, please simply restart the sound module by pressing any key.

In Europe, the dustbin symbol indicates that batteries, rechargeable batteries, button cells, battery packs, and similar materials must not be discarded in household waste. Batteries containing hazardous substances are harmful to the environment and to health. Please help to protect the environment from health risks by telling your children to dispose of batteries properly and by taking batteries to local collection points. Batteries handled in this manner are safely recycled.

Warning: Changes or modifications to this unit not expressly approved by the party responsible for compliance could void the user's authority to operate the equipment.

NOTE: This equipment has been tested and found to comply with the limits for a Class B digital device, pursuant to Part 15 of the FCC Rules. These limits are designed to provide reasonable protection against harmful interference in a residential installation. This equipment generates, uses, and can radiate radio frequency energy and, if not installed and used in accordance with the instructions, may cause harmful interference to radio communications. However, there is no guarantee that interference will not occur in a particular installation. If this equipment does cause harmful interference to radio or television reception, which can be determined by turning the equipment off and on, the user is encouraged to try to correct the interference by one or more of the following measures: Reorient or relocate the receiving antenna. Increase the separation between the equipment and receiver. Connect the equipment into an outlet on a circuit different from that to which the receiver is connected. Consult the dealer or an experienced radio TV technician for help.

Cover image sources: BX Space Exploration, PhotoDisc

Product and sound element design, engineering, and reproduction are proprietary technologies of Publications International, Ltd.

Published by Louis Weber, C.E.O., Publications International, Ltd.
7373 North Cicero Avenue
Lincolnwood, Illinois 60712

Ground Floor, 59 Gloucester Place
London W1U 8JJ

Customer Service: 1-888-724-0144 or customer_service@pilbooks.com

www.pilbooks.com

pil

Publications International, Ltd.

Manufactured in China.

8 7 6 5 4 3 2 1

ISBN-10: 1-60553-918-X
ISBN-13: 978-1-60553-918-8

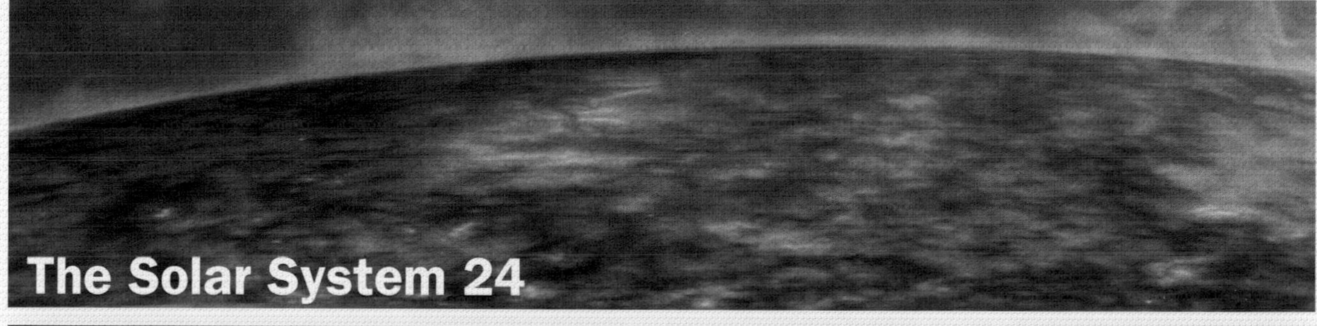

CHANGE THE VOLUME WITH THESE BUTTONS:

UP
DOWN

Destination: Other Worlds

The space age began in 1957 with the launching of the first artificial satellite. Since that time, *astronauts* and space probes have left the Earth to investigate space. To date, 12 men have visited the Moon. Advances in astronautics have made it possible to develop automatic *navigational systems* with which a spacecraft can reach and enter orbit around a planet. The Mars Express probe, launched in 2003 to take photographs of Mars, used this system. Mars Express, one of the *European Space Agency's* most productive missions around the Red Planet, is powered exclusively by solar energy.

SOLAR PANEL

FUEL TANKS

THRUSTER

Conventional Navigation

Navigational systems based on Earth require radio tracking.

The images taken are transmitted to Earth, and the navigational commands are sent to the spacecraft.

LAUNCH

Maneuvers are calculated on Earth, and the parameters are transmitted to the spacecraft.

2 Deploy

1 Launch

HIGH-GAIN ANTENNA

4 Transmission

3 Voyage

Space Programs

Unmanned

12 feet (3.7 m)

ARTIFICIAL SATELLITE IN POLAR ORBIT
Nimbus

89 feet (27 m)

METEOROLOGICAL SATELLITE
GOES

17 feet (5.1 m)

FLYBY SPACE PROBE
Mariner

4.3 feet (1.3 m)

ORBITING SPACE PROBE
Galileo

11 feet (3.3 m)

PROBE WITH A LANDING DEVICE
Viking

1 foot (0.3 m)

EXPLORATION VEHICLE
Sojourner

Space Walk

To gather more information, the astronauts conduct a space walk outside the spacecraft.

Manned

5 feet (1.5 m)

VOSTOK PROGRAM
Vostok 1

57.4 feet (17.5 m)

APOLLO PROGRAM
Apollo 11

11.5 feet (3.4 m)

GEMINI PROGRAM
Gemini 8

4.3 feet (1.3 m)

SPACE SHUTTLE
Columbia

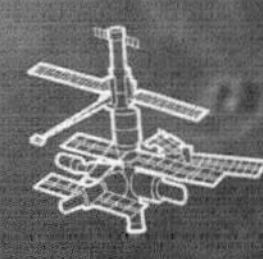

115 feet (35 m)

SPACE STATION
Mir

49 feet (15 m)

SPACE STATION
Skylab

From Fiction to Reality

Astronautics was born toward the end of the 19th century, when the Russian Konstantin Tsiolkovsky foresaw the ability of a *rocket* to overcome the force of gravity. Other pioneers were Hermann Oberth, who designed a liquid-fueled missile in 1917, which was later built by the American Robert Goddard in 1926. The German Wernher von Braun built the Redstone, Jupiter, and Saturn rockets, which made the manned landing on the Moon possible. Astronautics officially began in 1957 with the launching of the first artificial *satellite*, Sputnik 1. The second was Sputnik 2, which had on board the dog Laika.

SPUTNIK 1	
Launch	**October 1957**
Orbital altitude	**370 miles (600 km)**
Orbital period	**97 minutes**
Weight	**184 pounds (83.6 kg)**
Country	**USSR**

THE FIRST

Hermann Oberth
1894-1989
The scientist who worked on rocket technology during World War II.

THE SECOND

Robert Goddard
1882-1945
The U.S. physicist studied rockets and demonstrated their use for space travel.

THE THIRD

Wernher von Braun
1912-1977
The German physicist worked for Adolf Hitler designing ballistic missiles.

Sputnik 1

WEIGHT ON EARTH

184 pounds (83.6 kg)

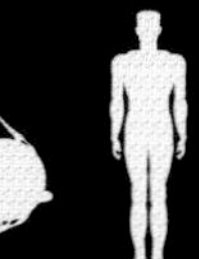

ANTENNAS

Sputnik 1 had four antennas between 7.9 and 9.5 feet (2.4-2.9 m) long.

1609
GALILEO

1798
CAVENDISH

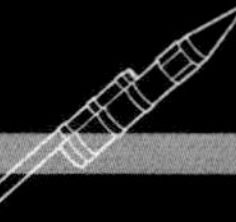
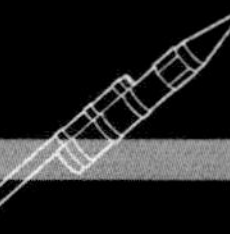

1806
ROCKETS

1838
DISTANCE

1926
THE FIRST ROCKET

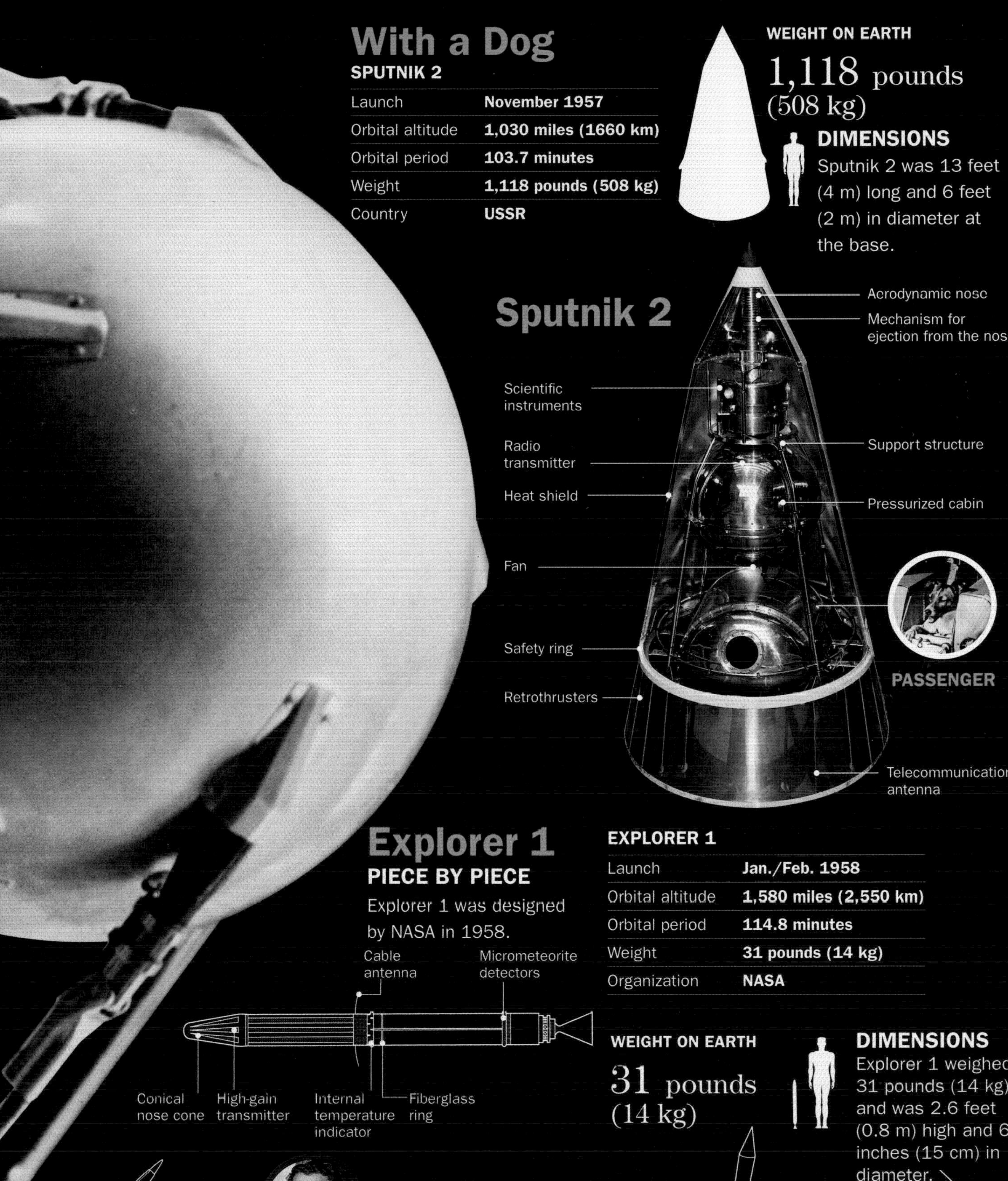

With a Dog
SPUTNIK 2
Launch November 1957
Orbital altitude 1,030 miles (1660 km)
Orbital period 103.7 minutes
Weight 1,118 pounds (508 kg)
Country USSR
WEIGHT ON EARTH
1,118 pounds (508 kg)
DIMENSIONS
Sputnik 2 was 13 feet (4 m) long and 6 feet (2 m) in diameter at the base.
Sputnik 2
Aerodynamic nose
Mechanism for ejection from the nose
Scientific instruments
Radio transmitter
Support structure
Heat shield
Pressurized cabin
Fan
Safety ring
PASSENGER
Retrothrusters
Telecommunications antenna
Explorer 1
PIECE BY PIECE
Explorer 1 was designed by NASA in 1958.
Cable antenna
Micrometeorite detectors
Conical nose cone
High-gain transmitter
Internal temperature indicator
Fiberglass ring
EXPLORER 1
Launch Jan./Feb. 1958
Orbital altitude 1,580 miles (2,550 km)
Orbital period 114.8 minutes
Weight 31 pounds (14 kg)
Organization NASA
WEIGHT ON EARTH
31 pounds (14 kg)
DIMENSIONS
Explorer 1 weighed 31 pounds (14 kg) and was 2.6 feet (0.8 m) high and 6 inches (15 cm) in diameter.

1927 ASSOCIATION

1932 VON BRAUN

1947 ROCKET PLANE

1949 BUMPER

1957 SPUTNIK 1

Russian Missions

After the initial successes with small *satellites*, where the effect of weightlessness was tested on animals, the Soviet Union, like the United States, began to develop programs for launching human beings into space. The first *astronaut* to orbit the Earth, at an altitude of 196 miles (315 km), was Yury Gagarin in 1961. He was the sole crew member of the Russian spacecraft Vostok 1. Gagarin orbited the Earth in his capsule, which was lifted into orbit by the SL-3 rocket and which had an ejection system for the cosmonaut in case of emergency.

Russians in Space

THE FIRST
Yury Gagarin
1934-68
The Russian cosmonaut h[illegible]d in promoting Russian astronautics. He died in a routine flight, on board a MiG-15 jet.

THE FIRST WOMAN
Valentina Tereshkova
(b. 1937)
Tereshkova was a parachute jumping enthusiast. It was not until 19 years later that another woman became a cosmonaut.

A WALK IN SPACE
Aleksey A. Leonov
(b. 1934)
In 1953 he joined the Air Force and in 1959 began training for spaceflight. In 1975 he commanded the Apollo-Soyuz mission.

VOSTOK 1	
Launch	**April 1961**
Orbital altitude	**196 miles (315 km)**
Orbital period	**1 hour, 48 minutes**
Weight	**5,400 pounds (2,460 kg)**
Country	**USSR**

WEIGHT ON EARTH

11,000 pounds
(5,000 kg)

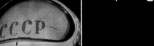

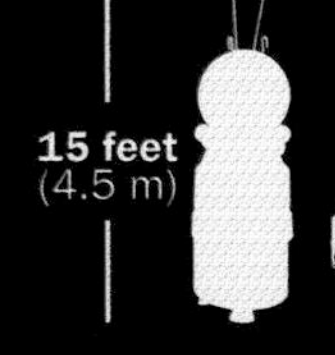
15 feet
(4.5 m)

ANTENNAS
It had powerful antennas to stay in contact with the Earth.

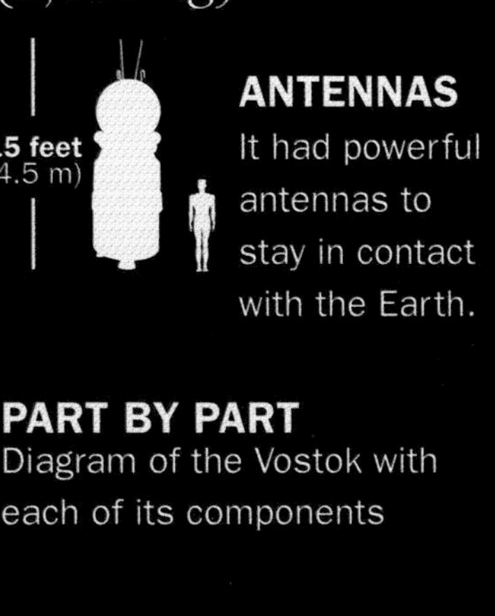

PART BY PART
Diagram of the Vostok with each of its components

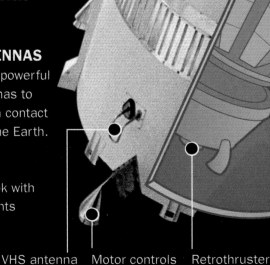

Inflatable air lock
Nitrogen and oxygen storage tanks
Access port
VHS antenna
Motor controls
Retrothruster

1957
SPUTNIK 2

1958
EXPLORER 1

NASA
1958
NASA

1959
LUNA 1

1959
LUNA 3

1960
LITTLE DOGS

Nitrogen storage tank

Cosmonaut

Cosmonaut ejection seat

VOSTOK PROGRAM

MISSIONS

Vostok 1	**April 12, 1961**
Vostok 2	**August 6, 1961**
Vostok 3	**August 11, 1962**
Vostok 4	**August 12, 1962**
Vostok 5	**June 14, 1963**
Vostok 6	**June 16, 1963**

VOSTOK BOOSTER ROCKET

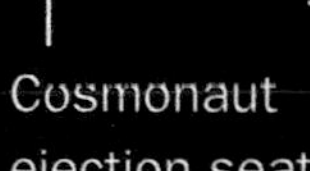

Manned module

FIRST STAGE | SECOND STAGE | THIRD STAGE

FIRST HUMAN

Return Ticket

1 LAUNCH

Liftoff

2 SEPARATION

3 EJECT

4 SEPARATE

5 LANDING

1961
HAM

1961
VOSTOK 1

1961
MERCURY

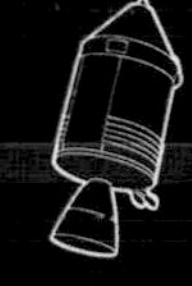

1964
GEMINI 1

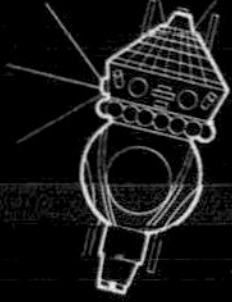

1964
VOSHKOD 1

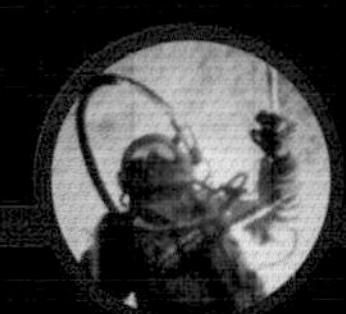

1965
VOSHKOD 2

North American Spacecraft

Over the course of the space race between the Soviet Union and the United States, the United States developed the Mercury program between 1959 and 1963. The manned capsule was small, with a volume of only 60 cubic feet (1.7 cu m). Before the first manned mission in May 1961, the American project sent three monkeys into space. The Mercury spacecraft were launched into space by two rockets: the Redstone, used for *suborbital flights*, and the Atlas, which was used in the five orbital flights that were achieved. Little Joe was used to test the escape tower and controls for aborting a mission.

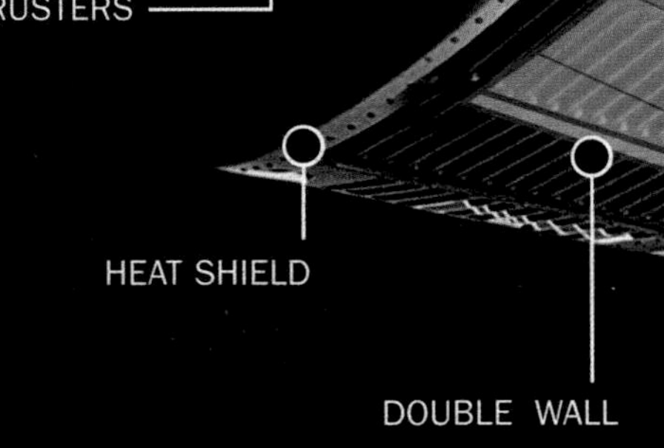
THRUSTERS
HEAT SHIELD
DOUBLE WALL

The Mercury Experience

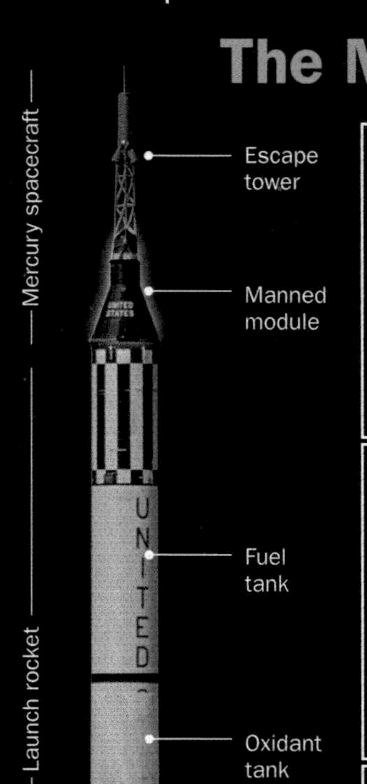
Mercury spacecraft
Launch rocket
Escape tower
Manned module
Fuel tank
Oxidant tank
Motor

TESTING

Ham

was the first monkey to fly into space. The spacecraft had sensors and remote-control instruments; Ham survived life in space without problems.

THE FIRST

Alan Shepard

1923-98

After his first voyage into space, he held important positions with NASA. In 1971 he was part of the Apollo 14 mission.

THE LAST

Gordon Cooper

1927-2004

Selected as an astronaut in 1959. In 1965 he carried out a Gemini mission that lasted 190 hours and 56 minutes. He retired in 1970.

MERCURY FLIGHTS

MERCURY WITH ANIMALS

Little Joe	**December 4, 1959**	Sam
Redstone	**January 31, 1961**	Ham
Atlas 5	**November 29, 1961**	Enos

MERCURY WITH ASTRONAUTS

Redstone 3	**May 5, 1961**	Alan Shepard
Redstone 4	**July 21, 1961**	Gus Grissom
Atlas 6	**February 20, 1962**	John Glenn
Atlas 7	**May 24, 1962**	Scott Carpente
Atlas 8	**October 3, 1962**	Wally Schirra
Atlas 9	**May 15, 1963**	Gordon Coope

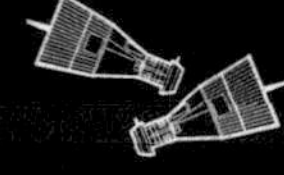
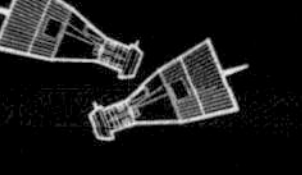

The Voyage

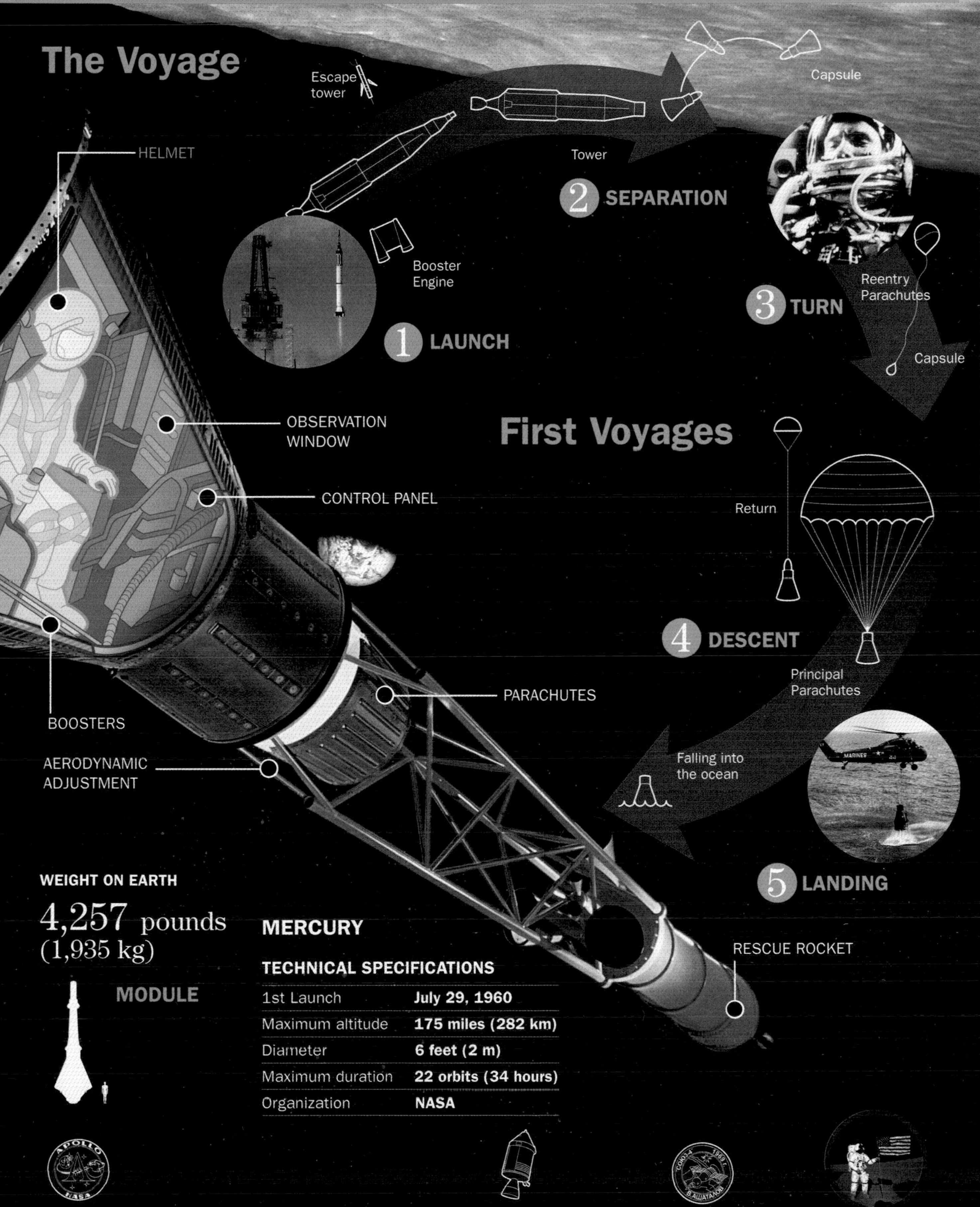
Escape tower
Tower
Capsule
Booster Engine
1 LAUNCH
2 SEPARATION
3 TURN
Reentry Parachutes
Capsule
Return
4 DESCENT
Principal Parachutes
Falling into the ocean
5 LANDING
HELMET
OBSERVATION WINDOW
CONTROL PANEL
BOOSTERS
AERODYNAMIC ADJUSTMENT
PARACHUTES
RESCUE ROCKET
MARINES

First Voyages

WEIGHT ON EARTH

4,257 pounds (1,935 kg)

MODULE

MERCURY

TECHNICAL SPECIFICATIONS

1st Launch	**July 29, 1960**
Maximum altitude	**175 miles (282 km)**
Diameter	**6 feet (2 m)**
Maximum duration	**22 orbits (34 hours)**
Organization	**NASA**

1966 APOLLO PROGRAM

1967 TRAGEDY

1967 SOYUZ 1

1968 APOLLO 8

1969 SOYUZ 4 AND 5

1969 APOLLO 11

A Giant Leap

The acceleration of the space race between the United States and the Soviet Union reached its height when President Kennedy's words set the goal of landing on the Moon before the end of the 1960s. In meeting that goal in 1969, a human being for the first time in history walked on the Moon. The mission took over a week, including the trip and the stay on the Moon. It was the first launch to use two boosters: one for leaving Earth to get to the Moon and the other to return from the Moon. Neil Armstrong was the first person to leave a human footprint and place a U.S. flag in outer space.

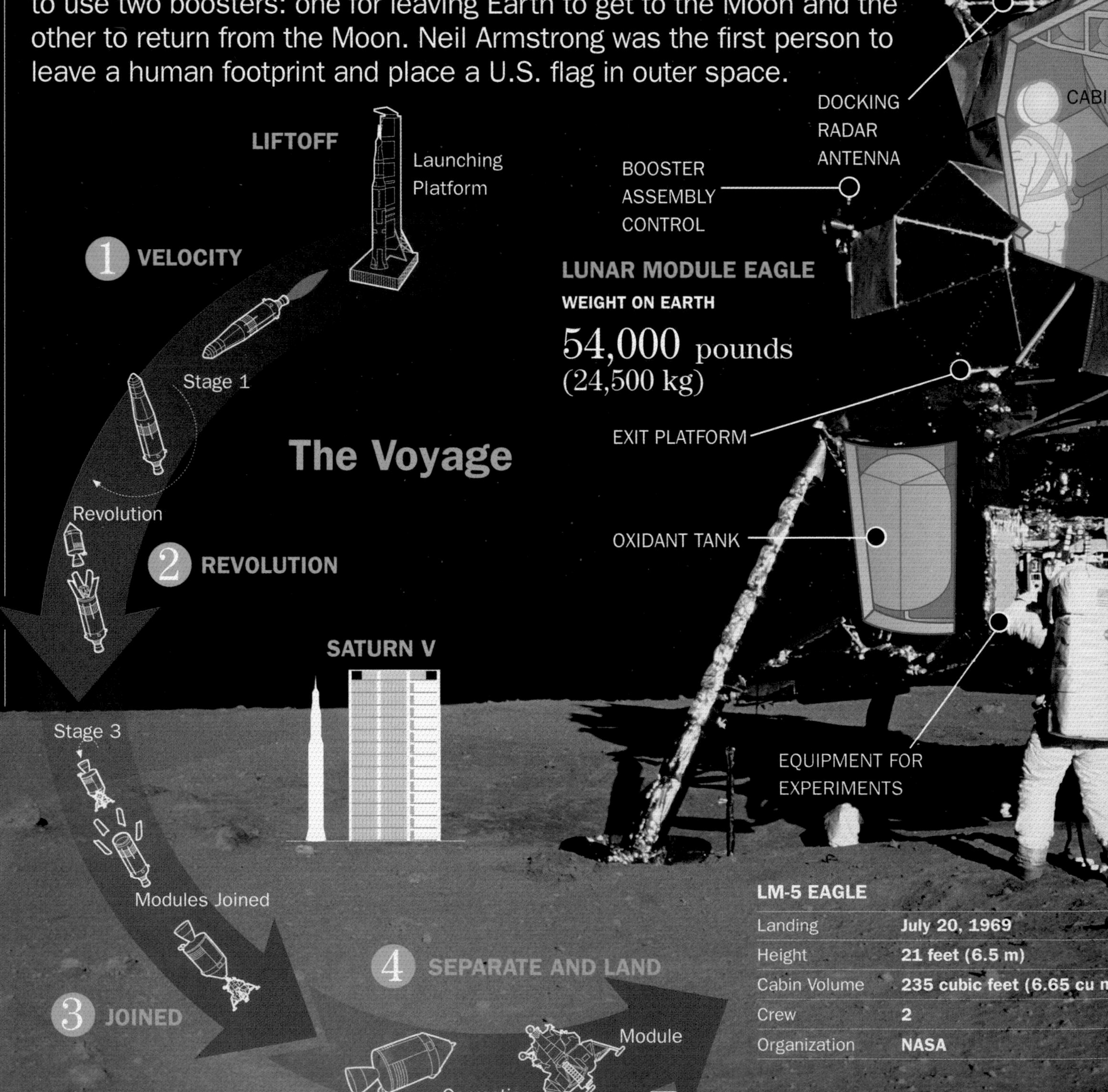
LIFTOFF
Launching Platform
1 VELOCITY
Stage 1
Revolution
2 REVOLUTION
The Voyage
SATURN V
Stage 3
Modules Joined
3 JOINED
4 SEPARATE AND LAND
Correction
Module
DOCKING RADAR ANTENNA
CABIN
BOOSTER ASSEMBLY CONTROL
LUNAR MODULE EAGLE
WEIGHT ON EARTH
54,000 pounds (24,500 kg)
EXIT PLATFORM
OXIDANT TANK
EQUIPMENT FOR EXPERIMENTS

LM-5 EAGLE

Landing	July 20, 1969
Height	21 feet (6.5 m)
Cabin Volume	235 cubic feet (6.65 cu m
Crew	2
Organization	NASA

The Modules

MANEUVERABLE ANTENNA

OXYGEN TANKS FOR THRUST

ULTRA HIGH-FREQUENCY ANTENNA

FUEL TANK

LANDING GEAR

ENORMOUS EAGLE

ORBITAL MODULE

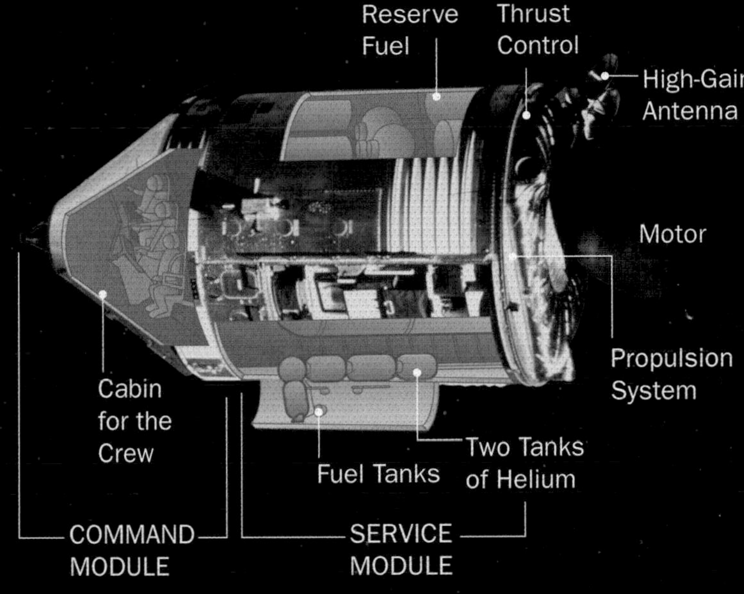
Reserve Fuel
Thrust Control
High-Gain Antenna
Motor
Propulsion System
Cabin for the Crew
Fuel Tanks
Two Tanks of Helium
COMMAND MODULE
SERVICE MODULE

CSM-107 COLUMBIA

Launch	**July 16, 1969**
Height	**36 feet (11 m)**
Diameter	**12.8 feet (3.9 m)**
Cabin volume	**220 cubic feet (6.2 cu m)**
Crew	**3**
Organization	**NASA**

WEIGHT ON EARTH

66,000 pounds (30,000 kg)

The Crew

Neil Armstrong (b. 1930) carried out his first mission on board Gemini 8 in 1966. He was the first person to set foot on the Moon. He retired from NASA in 1971.	**Michael Collins** (b. 1930) was the third astronaut to carry out a space walk with the Gemini 10 mission. He was the command module pilot of the Columbia.	**Edwin Aldrin** (b. 1930) took part in the Gemini 13 training mission and was the second man to set foot on lunar soil.

The Moon Without Secrets

Six Apollo missions were able to land on the lunar surface. Apollo 13, because of an oxygen-tank explosion, flew to the Moon but did not make a landing. Through the intelligence and expertise of the *astronauts* onboard, it was able to return to Earth safely. With the success of these missions, the Moon was no longer unreachable. A dozen men were able to walk on the gray, crunchy lava soil strewn with craters. Each one of these voyages, besides bringing back data, encouraged the development of space science and increased the desire to carry out other missions to different locations of the solar system.

The Apollo Missions

TWENTY-ONE CHOSEN

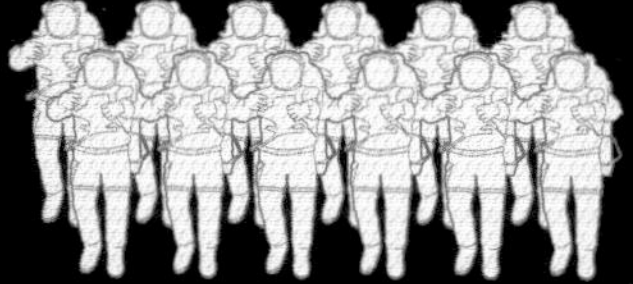

LUNAR MATERIAL

740 pounds (336 kg)

DISTANCE TRAVELED

15.5 miles (25 km)

STAY

301 h 51 m 50 s

HAPPY ENDING

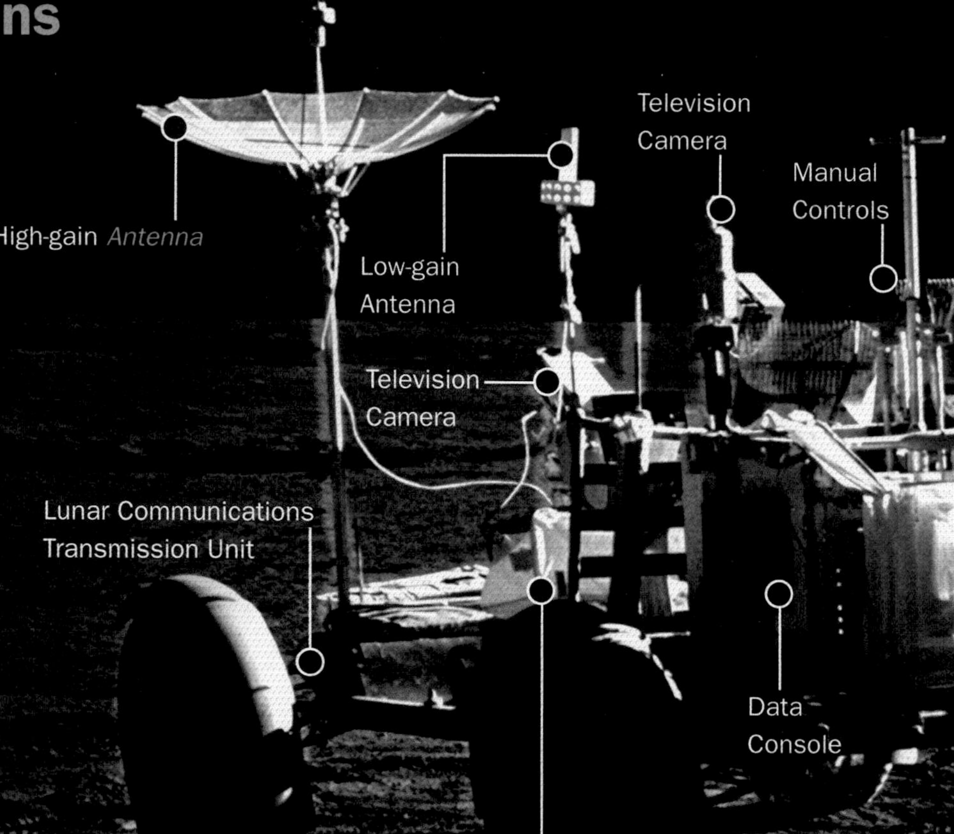
High-gain *Antenna*
Low-gain Antenna
Television Camera
Television Camera
Manual Controls
Lunar Communications Transmission Unit
Data Console
Storage Locker

THE LUNAR ROVER
An electric vehicle used by the astronauts to explore the surface of the moon.

APOLLO MISSIONS

1970
APOLLO 13

1972
SAMPLES

1975
APOLLO-SOYUZ

Lunar Prospector Mission

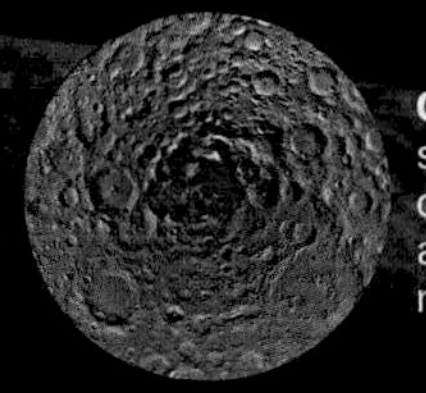

LUNAR POLE
Images taken by the Lunar Prospector

LUNAR PROSPECTOR

Gamma-Ray Spectrometer searches for potassium, oxygen, uranium, aluminum, silicon, calcium, magnesium, and titanium.

Solar Sensors

Antenna used to maintain communications with the Earth.

Magnetometer looks for magnetic fields near the spacecraft.

Thrusters

Solar Panel

Alpha Particle Spectrometer detects particles emitted by radioactive gases.

Neutron Spectrometer detects neutrons on the lunar surface.

LUNAR PROSPECTOR	
Launch	**January 1998**
Flight to the Moon	**105 hours**
Weight	**650 pounds (295 kg)**
Cost	**$63 million**
Organization	**NASA**

ANTENNAS
Permit communication with NASA's Deep Space network.

End of the Apollo Program

LUNAR ROVER	
Launch	**July 1971**
Length	**10.2 feet (3.1 m)**
Width	**3.7 feet (1.14 m)**
Velocity	**10 mph (16 km/h)**
Organization	**NASA**

ANTENNAS
High-gain, in the form of an umbrella on the Lunar Rover

WEIGHT ON EARTH

406 pounds (209 kg)

WEIGHT ON THE MOON

77 pounds (35 kg)

ample
ollection Bag

APOLLO 13
James A. Lovell, Jr.
(b. 1928)
was the backup commander for the Gemini 4 flight and command pilot of Gemini 7 and 12.

SCIENTIST
Harrison Schmitt
(b. 1928)
North American geologist who flew on the last Apollo mission

APOLLO-SOYUZ
Aleksey Leonov
(b. 1934)
was born in Siberia. During the Voshkod 2 mission, he was the first person to walk in space.

LATER MISSIONS

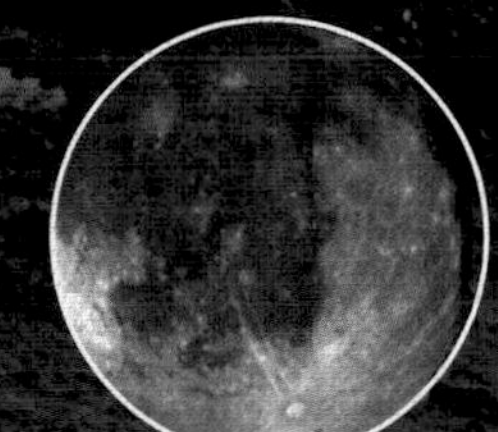

1994
CLEMENTINE

2003
SMART

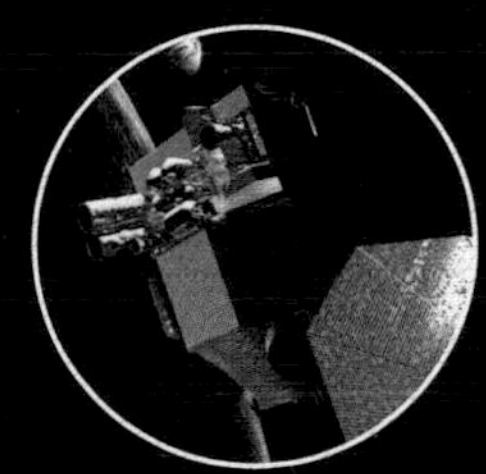

2009
LRO

The Rockets

Developed in the first half of the 20th century, *rockets* are necessary for sending any kind of object into space. They produce sufficient force to leave the ground together with their cargo and in a short time acquire the velocity necessary to reach orbit in space around the Earth. On average, more than one rocket per week is sent into space from somewhere in the world.

ARIANE 5

First operational flight	**October 11, 1999**
Diameter	**16 feet (50 m)**
Total height	**167 feet (51 m)**
Booster rocket weight	**610,000 pounds (277,000 kg) each (full)**
Geosynchronous payload	**15,000 pounds (6,800 kg)**
Organization	**ESA**

Boeing
Space Shuttle
Ariane 5

1,645,000 pounds
(746,000 kg)
WEIGHT OF ARIANE 5

CONICAL NOSE CONE protects the cargo.

UPPER ***PAYLOAD*** Up to two satellites.

LOWER ***PAYLOAD*** Up to two satellites.

LIQUID OXYGEN TANK contains 286,000 pounds (130,000 kg) for combustion.

UPPER ENGINES release the *satellite* at a precise angle and speed.

COMPONENTS

Payload System

Guidance System

Propulsion System

ACCORDING TO THE FUEL TYPE THEY USE, THESE WOULD BE CONSIDERED CHEMICAL (FUEL) ROCKETS.

KEY Gases Expelled

LIQUID **SOLID** **HYBRID**

Engine Operation

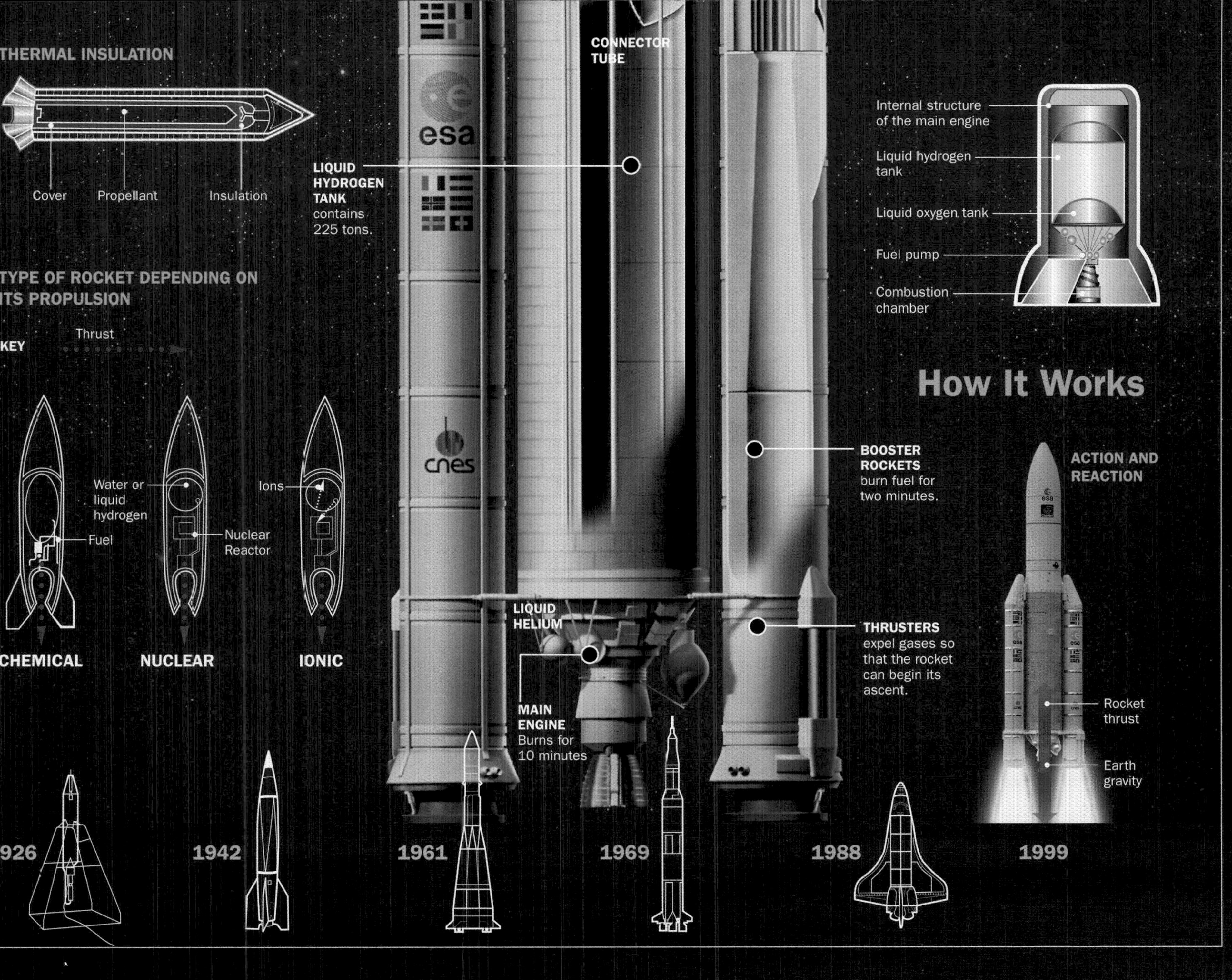
How It Works
THERMAL INSULATION
Cover
Propellant
Insulation
TYPE OF ROCKET DEPENDING ON ITS PROPULSION
KEY
Thrust
Water or liquid hydrogen
Fuel
Nuclear Reactor
Ions
CHEMICAL
NUCLEAR
IONIC
LIQUID HYDROGEN TANK contains 225 tons.
CONNECTOR TUBE
esa
cnes
LIQUID HELIUM
MAIN ENGINE Burns for 10 minutes
BOOSTER ROCKETS burn fuel for two minutes.
THRUSTERS expel gases so that the rocket can begin its ascent.
Internal structure of the main engine
Liquid hydrogen tank
Liquid oxygen tank
Fuel pump
Combustion chamber
ACTION AND REACTION
Rocket thrust
Earth gravity
1926
1942
1961
1969
1988
1999

Space Shuttle

Unlike conventional *rockets*, the U.S. space shuttle can be reused to lift *satellites* into space and put them into low Earth orbit. Today these vehicles are also used to make flights to the International Space Station. The U.S. fleet has three shuttles: *Discovery*, *Atlantis*, and *Endeavour*. The *Challenger* exploded in 1986 and the *Columbia* in 2003.

TECHNICAL DATA FOR THE SPACE SHUTTLE

First launch	**April 12-14, 1981**
Mission length	**5-20 days**
Width	**79 feet (24 m)**
Length	**121 feet (37 m)**
Organization	**NASA**

WEIGHT ON EARTH

25,500 pounds
(11,600 kg)

External fuel tank

Space orbiter

Auxiliary rockets

SATELLITE

ROBOT ARM

SPACE ORBITER

COMMAND CABIN

CERAMICS

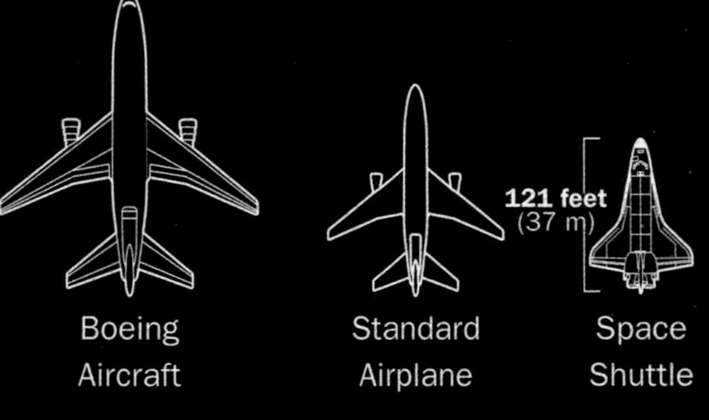
121 feet
(37 m)
Boeing Aircraft
Standard Airplane
Space Shuttle

The Cabin

CONTROLS

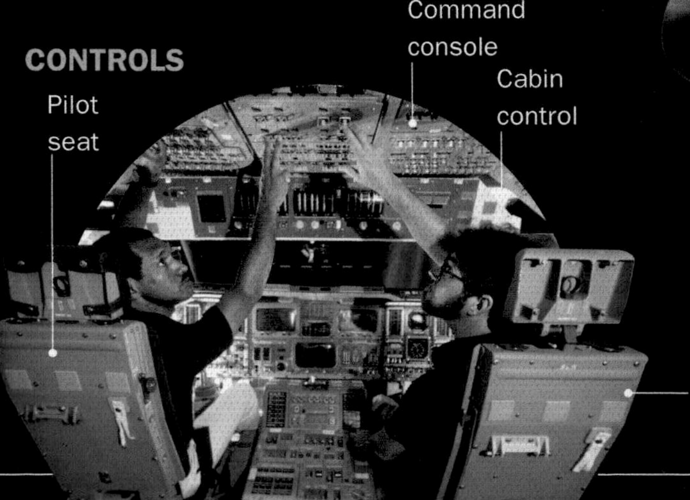
Pilot seat
Command console
Cabin control
Commander's chair

Adhesive ceramic fiber

Protective felt

Glass covering

Silicon ceramic tiles

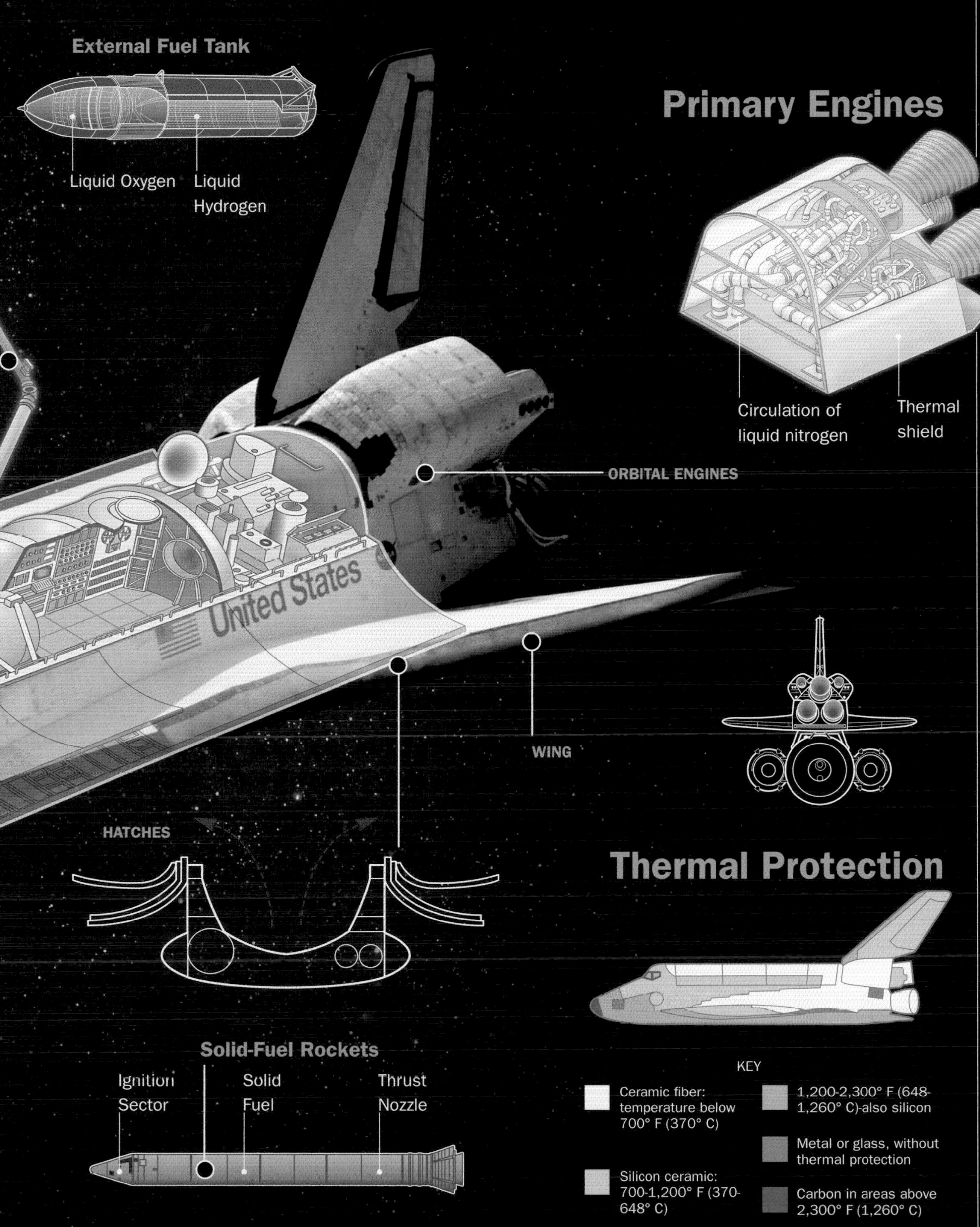
External Fuel Tank
Liquid Oxygen
Liquid Hydrogen
Primary Engines
Circulation of liquid nitrogen
Thermal shield
ORBITAL ENGINES
United States
WING
HATCHES
Thermal Protection
Solid-Fuel Rockets
Ignition Sector
Solid Fuel
Thrust Nozzle
KEY
Ceramic fiber: temperature below 700° F (370° C)
Silicon ceramic: 700-1,200° F (370-648° C)
1,200-2,300° F (648-1,260° C)-also silicon
Metal or glass, without thermal protection
Carbon in areas above 2,300° F (1,260° C)

Profession: Astronaut

How do you become an astronaut? Before undertaking a mission in space, every candidate must submit to rigorous examinations since the tasks they are to perform are very delicate and risky. They must intensively study mathematics, meteorology, astronomy, and physics and become familiar with computers and navigation in space. They must also train physically to get used to low-gravity conditions in orbit and to be able to carry out repairs.

Manned Maneuvering Unit

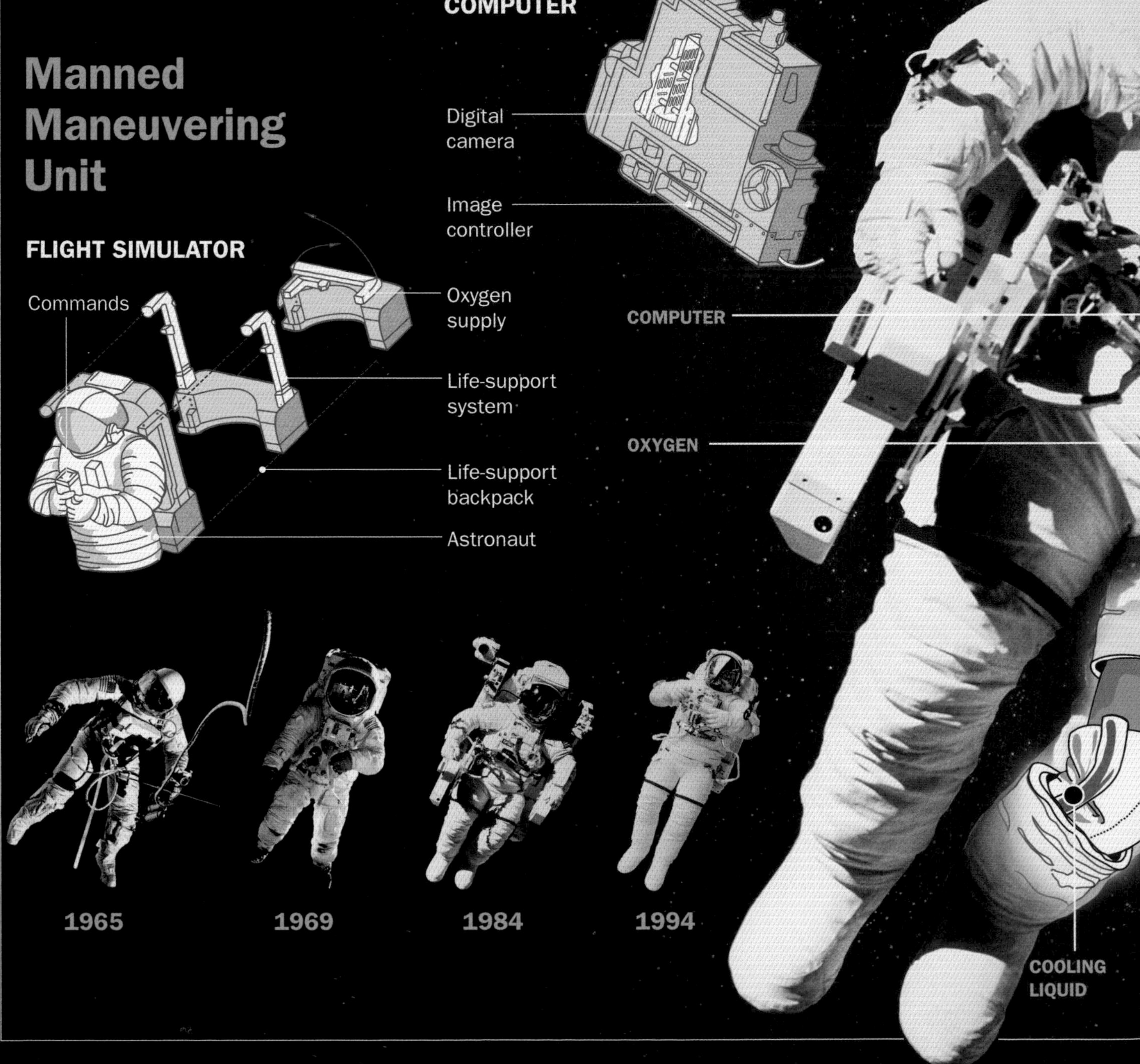
COMPUTER
Digital camera
Image controller
FLIGHT SIMULATOR
Commands
Oxygen supply
Life-support system
Life-support backpack
Astronaut
COMPUTER
OXYGEN
1965
1969
1984
1994
COOLING LIQUID

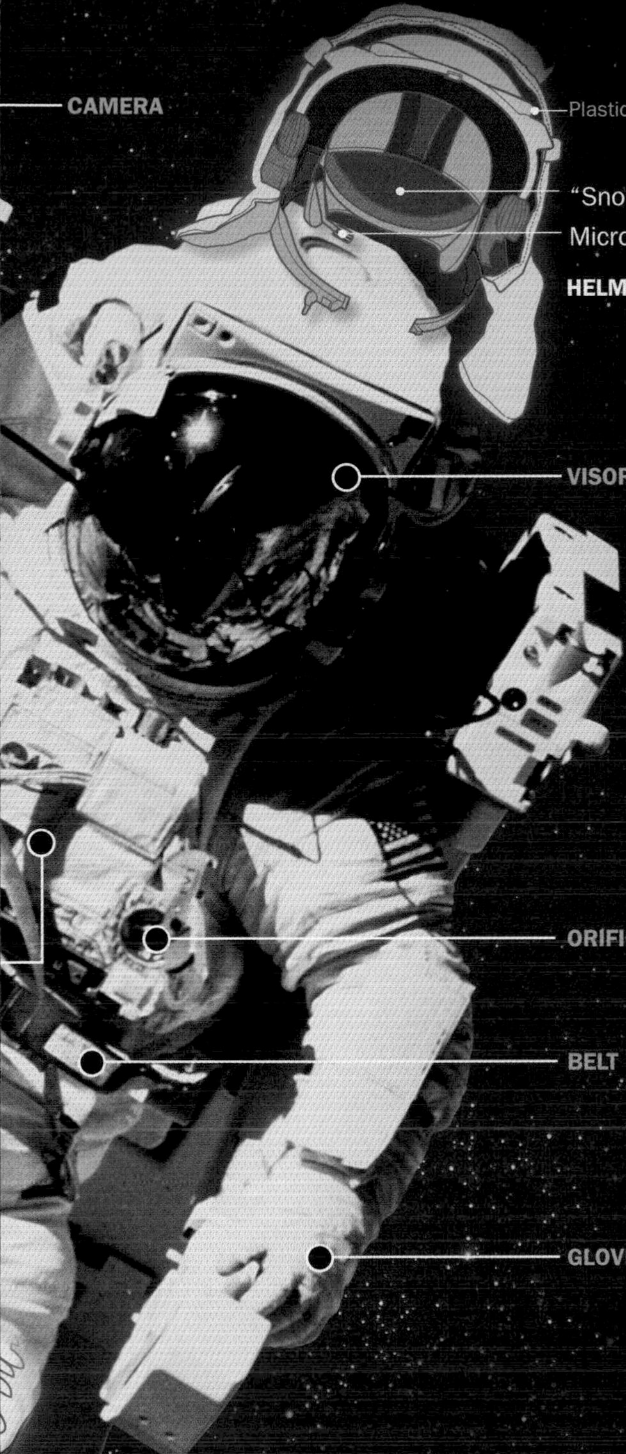

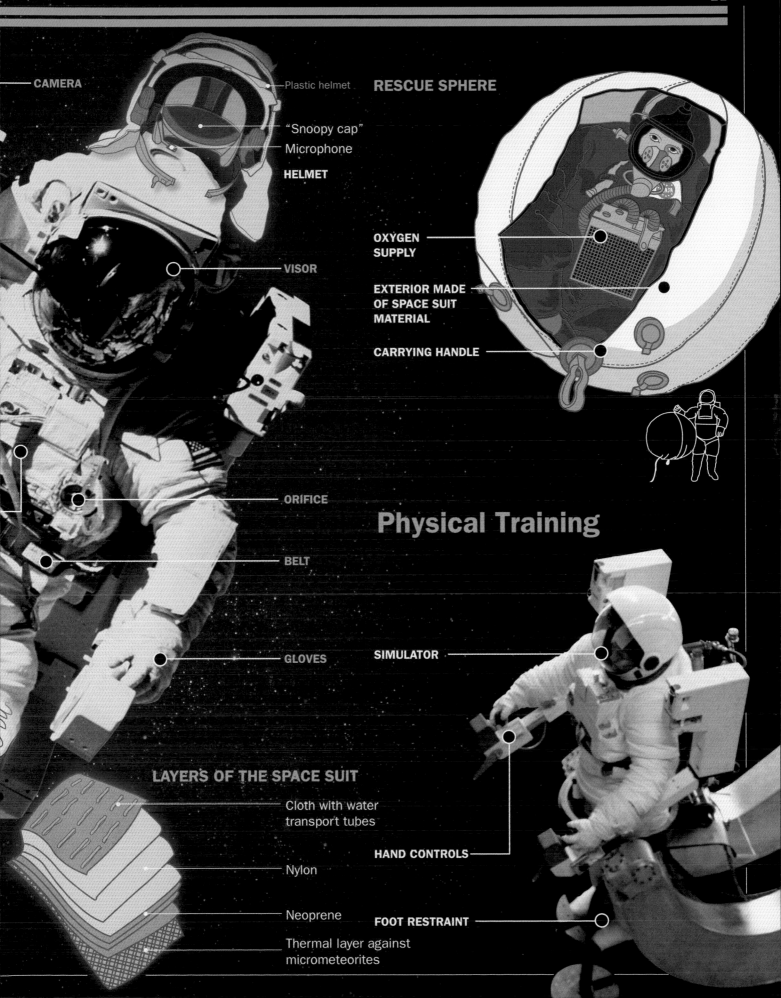

CAMERA

Plastic helmet

"Snoopy cap"

Microphone

HELMET

VISOR

ORIFICE

BELT

GLOVES

RESCUE SPHERE

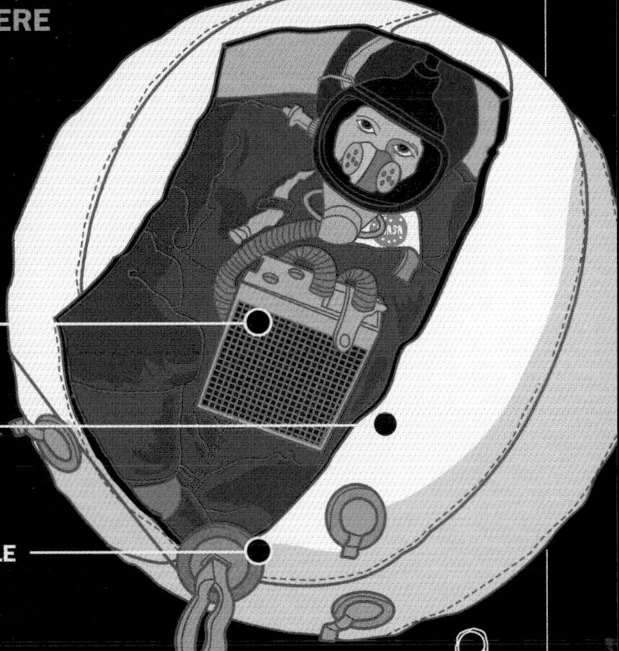

OXYGEN SUPPLY

EXTERIOR MADE OF SPACE SUIT MATERIAL

CARRYING HANDLE

Physical Training

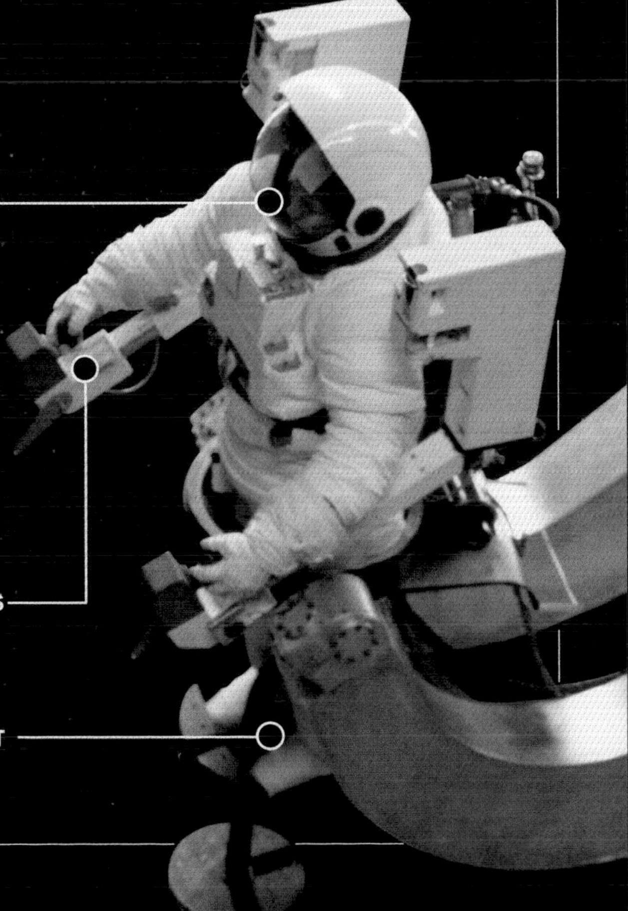

SIMULATOR

HAND CONTROLS

FOOT RESTRAINT

LAYERS OF THE SPACE SUIT

Cloth with water transport tubes

Nylon

Neoprene

Thermal layer against micrometeorites

Space Probes

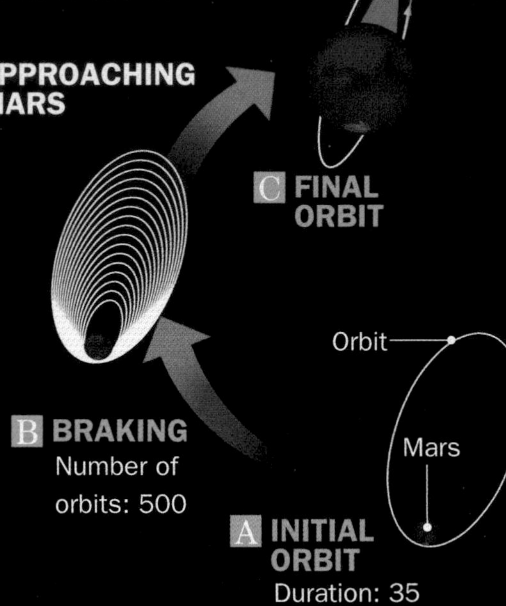
APPROACHING MARS
C FINAL ORBIT
Orbit
Mars
B BRAKING
Number of orbits: 500
A INITIAL ORBIT
Duration: 35

From the first spacecraft, such as Mariner of the mid-1960s, to the Mars Reconnaissance Orbiter launched in 2005 for a close-up study of Mars, *space probes* have made major contributions. Most of them have been solar-powered; they are the size of an automobile, and they travel to predetermined locations using rockets for thrust. These unmanned machines are equipped with cameras, sensors, *spectrometers*, and other sophisticated instruments that allow them to study the planets, moons, comets, and asteroids in detail.

Mars Reconnaissance Orbiter (MRO)

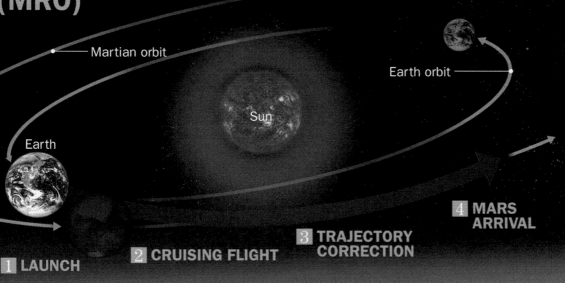

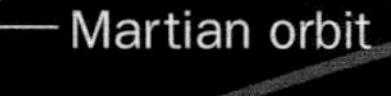

Martian orbit

Earth orbit

Mars

Sun

Earth

1 LAUNCH

2 CRUISING FLIGHT

3 TRAJECTORY CORRECTION

4 MARS ARRIVAL

5 SCIENTIFIC PHASE

TECHNICAL DATA FOR THE SPACE SHUTTLE

Weight with fuel	**4,800 pounds (2,180)**
Temperature rating of the panels	**Down to -390° F (-200° C)**
Launch rocket	**Atlas V-401**
Mission duration	**Five years (with possible extension)**
Cost	**$720 million**

WEIGHT ON EARTH

2,270 pounds (1,031 kg)

72 million miles (116 million km)

THE DISTANCE TRAVELED BY THE PROBE TO REACH MARS

Arrival

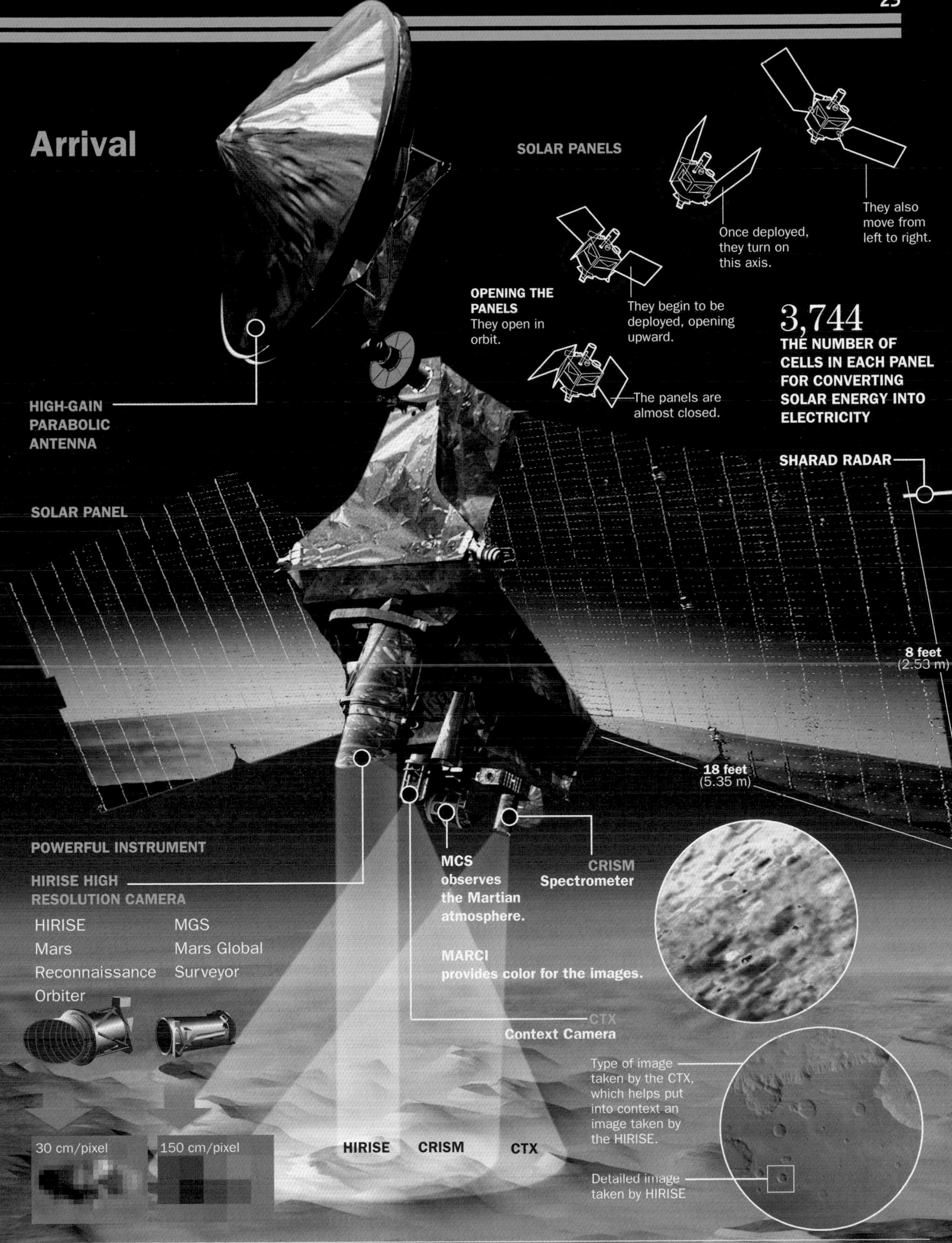

SOLAR PANELS
OPENING THE PANELS
They open in orbit.
The panels are almost closed.
They begin to be deployed, opening upward.
Once deployed, they turn on this axis.
They also move from left to right.
3,744
THE NUMBER OF CELLS IN EACH PANEL FOR CONVERTING SOLAR ENERGY INTO ELECTRICITY
HIGH-GAIN PARABOLIC ANTENNA
SOLAR PANEL
SHARAD RADAR
8 feet (2.53 m)
18 feet (5.35 m)
POWERFUL INSTRUMENT
HIRISE HIGH RESOLUTION CAMERA
HIRISE
Mars Reconnaissance Orbiter
MGS
Mars Global Surveyor
MCS
observes the Martian atmosphere.
CRISM
Spectrometer
MARCI
provides color for the images.
CTX
Context Camera
Type of image taken by the CTX, which helps put into context an image taken by the HIRISE.
Detailed image taken by HIRISE
30 cm/pixel
150 cm/pixel
HIRISE
CRISM
CTX

Attracted by a Star

Planets and their satellites, *asteroids* and other rocky objects, and an incalculable number of cometlike objects, some more than 1 trillion miles (1.6 trillion km) from the Sun, make up the solar system. In the 17th century, astronomer Johannes Kepler proposed a model to interpret the dynamic properties of the bodies of the solar system. According to this interpretation, the planets complete *elliptical* trajectories, called orbits, around the Sun. In every case, the movement is produced by the influence of the *gravitational* field of the Sun. Today, as part of a rapidly developing field of astronomy, it is known that planet or planetlike bodies also orbit other stars.

Outer Planets

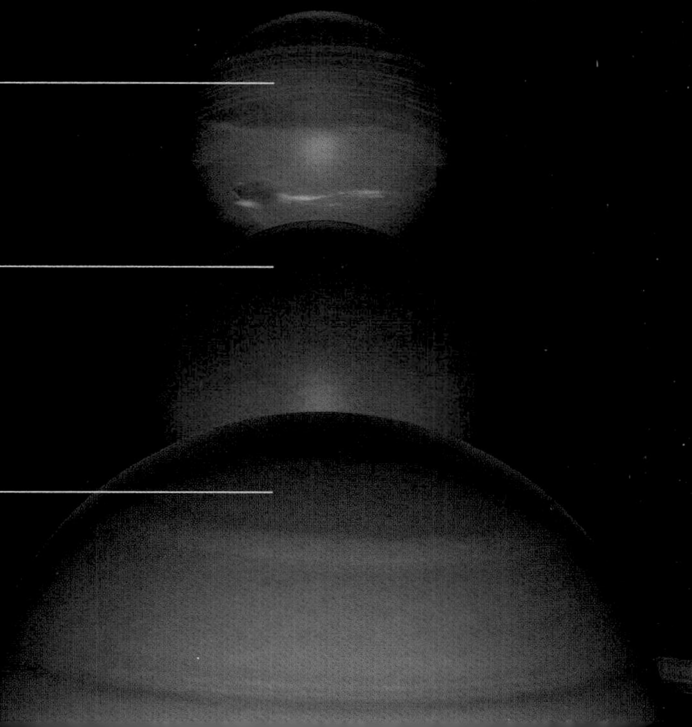

NEPTUNE
DIAMETER 30,775 MILES (49,528 km)
MOONS 13

Triton Proteus Nereid

URANUS
DIAMETER 31,763 MILES (51,118 km)
MOONS 27

Titania Oberon Umbriel Ariel Miranda Puck

SATURN
DIAMETER 74,898 MILES (120,536 km)
MOONS 50+

Titan Rhea Iapetus Tethys

ORBITS

Earth's orbit
Venus's orbit
Mercury's orbit
Mars's orbit
Main belt
Jupiter's orbit
Saturn's orbit
Uranus's orbit
Neptune's orbit

The rotation of most planets around their own axes is in counterclockwise direction. Venus and Uranus, however, revolve clockwise.

JUPITER
DIAMETER 88,846 MILES (142,984 km)
MOONS 60+

Ganymede Callisto Io Europa

BUILDING PLANETS

1 ORIGIN

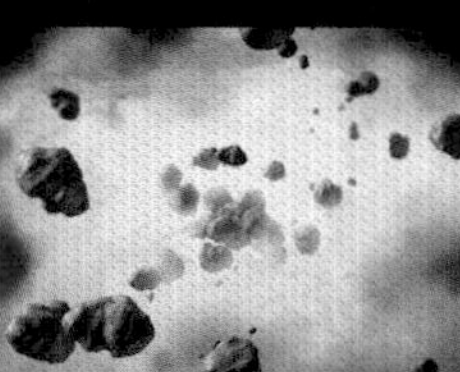

2 COLLISION

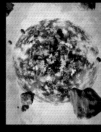

3 HEAT

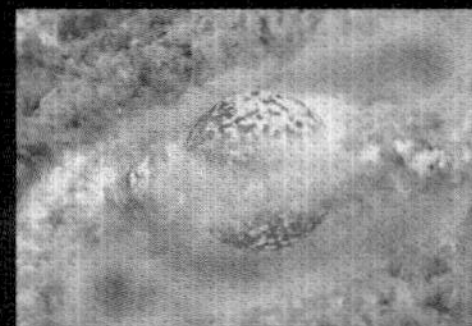

Asteroid Belt

Inner Planets

Phobos Deimos

MARS
DIAMETER 4,217 MILES (6,786 km)
MOCNS 2

EARTH
DIAMETER 7,926 MILES (12,756 km)
MOCNS 1

Moon

VENUS
DIAMETER 7,520 MILES (12,103 km)
MOONS 0

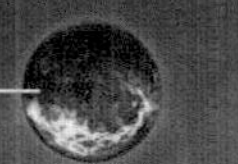

MERCURY
DIAMETER 3,031 MILES (4,878 km)
MOCNS 0

SOLAR GRAVITY

SUN

A Very Warm Heart

The Sun at the center of the solar system is a source of light and heat. This energy is produced by the fusion of atomic *hydrogen* nuclei, which generate *helium* nuclei. The energy that emanates from the Sun travels through space and initially encounters the bodies that populate the solar system. The Sun shines thanks to *thermonuclear fusion*, and it will continue to shine until its supply of hydrogen runs out in about six or seven billion years.

The Sun

CHARACTERISTICS

CONVENTIONAL SYMBOL

ESSENTIAL DATA

Average distance from Earth	93 million miles (150 million km)
Equatorial diameter	864,000 miles (1,391,000 km)
Orbital speed	7,456 miles per second (12,000 km/s)
*Mass**	332,900
*Gravity**	28
Density	0.81 ounce per cubic inch (1.4 g per cu cm)
Average temperature	9,932° F (5,500° C)
Atmosphere	Dense

*In both cases, Earth = 1

1 NUCLEAR COLLISION
CONVECTIVE ZONE
RADIATIVE ZONE
Proton
Positron
Neutron
Neutrin
Deuterium
Photon
2 PHOTONS
Deuterium 1
NUCLEAR FUSION OF HYDROGEN
HELIUM NUCLEUS
Deuterium 2
3 HELIUM NUCLEI
Proton 1
Proton 2

Surface and Atmosphere

SUNSPOTS

PENUMBRA
Peripheral region. It is the hottest and brightest part of the sun.

UMBRA
Central region. It is the coldest and darkest part.

PHOTOSPHERE

10,112° F
(5,600° C)

CORE

27,000,000° F
(15,000,000° C)

CHROMOSPHERE

SPICULES

MACROSPICULES

CORONA

1,800,000° F
(1,000,000° C)
THE TEMPERATURE IN THE *CORONA*

SOLAR WIND

SOLAR PROMINENCES

SOLAR FLARES

Solar Winds

A natural spectacle of incomparable beauty, the *auroras* are produced around the magnetic poles of the Earth by the activity of the Sun. Solar wind acts on the *magnetosphere*, which is a part of the exosphere. In general, the greater the solar wind, the more prominent the *aurora*. Auroras consist of luminous patches and columns of various colors. Depending on whether they appear in the north or south, they are called aurora borealis or aurora australis. The aurora borealis can be seen in Alaska, Canada, and the Scandinavian countries.

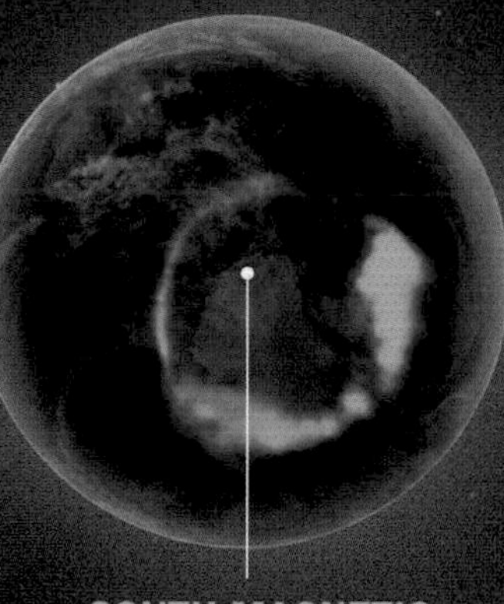
SOUTH MAGNETIC POLE

Solar Winds

SOLAR WIND
Bow Shock Wave
Magnetotail

How They Are Produced

620 miles (1,000 km)

is how long an aurora can be. From space it will look like a circle around one of the magnetic poles of the Earth.

Sodium atoms and *molecules*
Nitrogen atoms and *molecules*
310-370 miles (500-600 km) Magnetosphere (Exosphere)
0-6 miles (0-10 km) Troposphere
0 miles (km)
55-300 miles (90-500 km) Mesosphere
62 miles (100 km)
Oxygen atoms and *molecules*
250 miles (400 km)

1 ELECTRONS COLLIDE WITH MOLECULES

2 THEY BECOME EXCITED

3 THEY GENERATE LIGHT

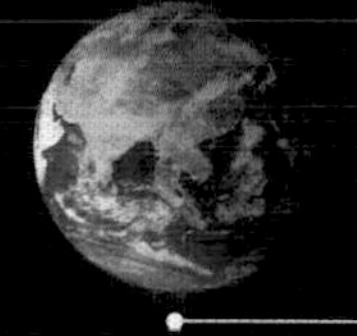

THE EARTH
THE POLES
Oval Aurora

10-20 minutes

DURATION OF THE PHENOMENON

The amount of light emitted oscillates between 1 and 10 million megawatts, equivalent to the energy produced by 1,000 to 10,000 large electric power plants.

Closer to the Sun

The *space probe* Ulysses was launched from the *space shuttle* on Oct. 6, 1990. It completed its first orbit around the Sun in 1997 and since then has carried out one of the most in-depth studies ever about our star. The probe's orbits allow it to study the *heliosphere* at all latitudes, from the equator to the poles, in both the northern and southern hemispheres of the Sun. The joint *NASA* and *ESA* mission is the first to orbit around the poles of the Sun. It orbits the Sun at 10 miles per second (15.4 km/s).

PASSES OVER THE SOLAR NORTH POLE
June-October 1995
September-December 2001
November 2007-January 2008

1 Beginning of the first orbit: **1992**

2 Beginning of the second orbit: **1998**

3 Beginning of the third orbit: **2004**

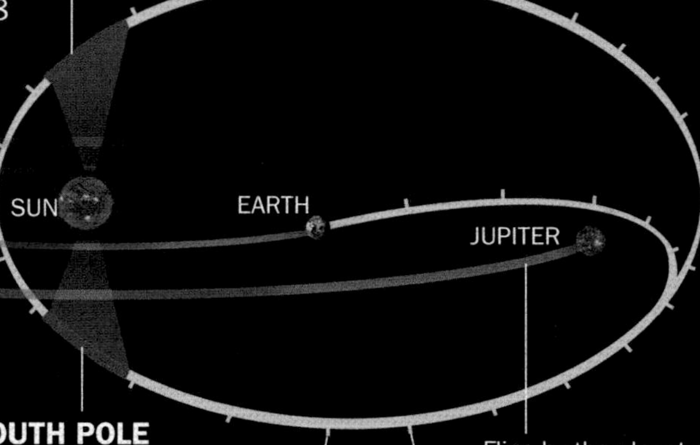
SUN
EARTH
JUPITER

PASSES OVER THE SOLAR SOUTH POLE
June-November 1994 / September 2000
January 2001 / November 2006-April 2007

100 days

Flies by the planet and uses it for a gravity assist

FIRST ORBIT

ORDER OF THE HELIOSPHERE

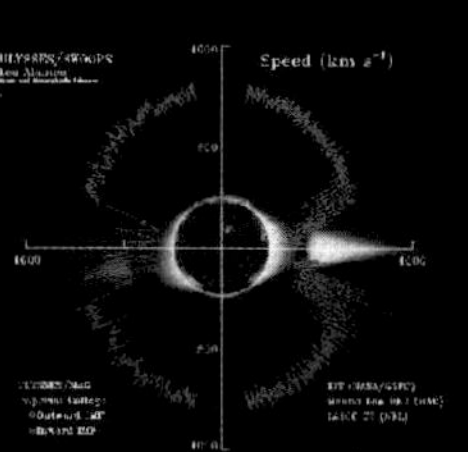

SECOND ORBIT

HELIOSPHERE CHAOS

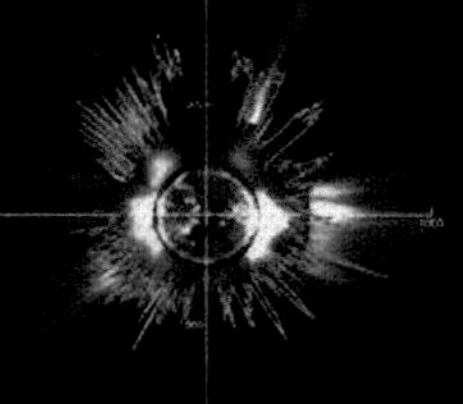

THIRD ORBIT

CHANGES IN THE MAGNETIC FIELD

HIGH-GAIN *ANTENNA*

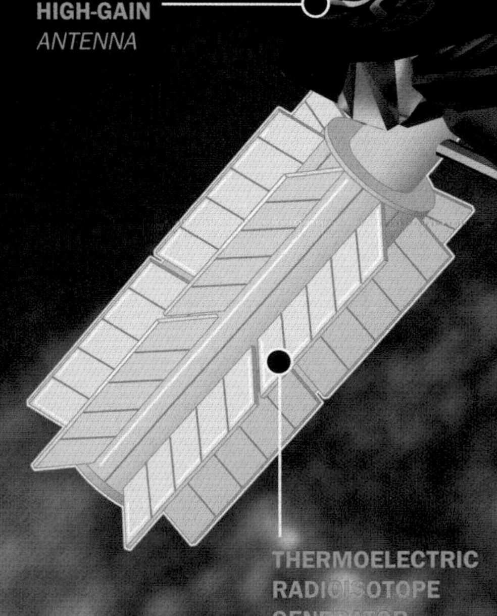

THERMOELECTRIC RADIOISOTOPE GENERATOR

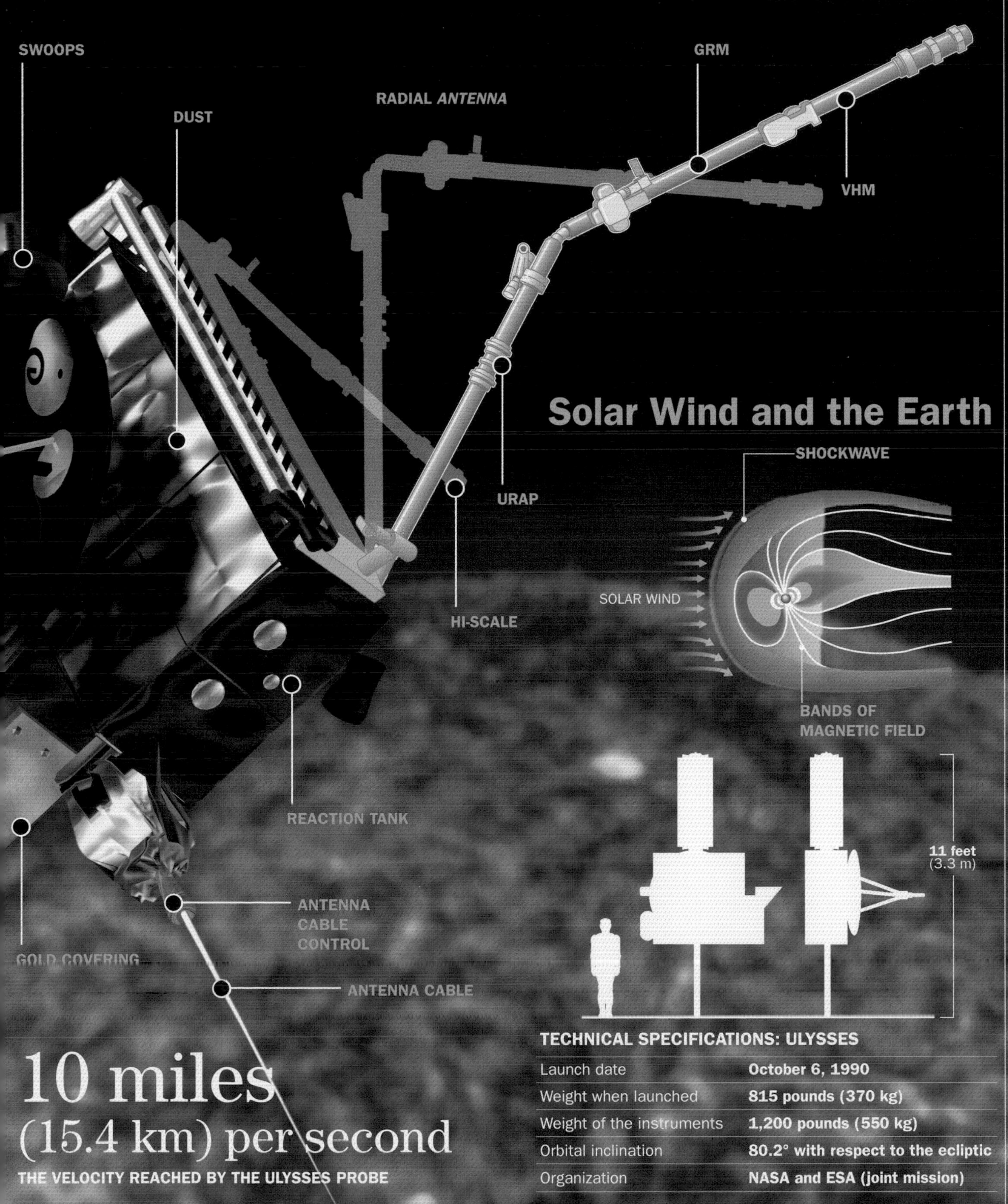
SWOOPS
DUST
RADIAL ANTENNA
GRM
VHM
URAP
HI-SCALE
REACTION TANK
ANTENNA CABLE CONTROL
GOLD COVERING
ANTENNA CABLE
SHOCKWAVE
SOLAR WIND
BANDS OF MAGNETIC FIELD
11 feet
(3.3 m)

Solar Wind and the Earth

TECHNICAL SPECIFICATIONS: ULYSSES

Launch date	**October 6, 1990**
Weight when launched	**815 pounds (370 kg)**
Weight of the instruments	**1,200 pounds (550 kg)**
Orbital inclination	**80.2° with respect to the ecliptic**
Organization	**NASA and ESA (joint mission)**

10 miles (15.4 km) per second

THE VELOCITY REACHED BY THE ULYSSES PROBE

Mercury, an Inferno

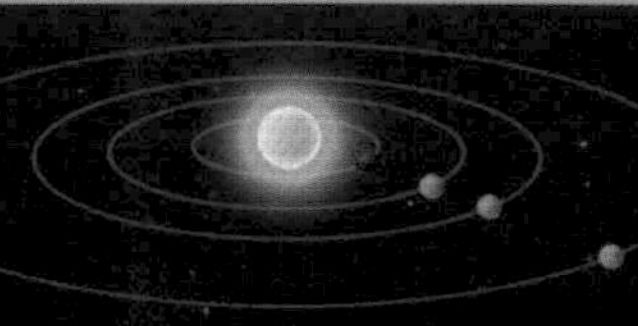

Mercury is the planet nearest to the Sun and is therefore the one that has to withstand the harshest of the Sun's effects. Due to its proximity to the Sun, Mercury moves at great speed in its solar orbit, completing an orbit every 88 days. It has almost no *atmosphere*, and its surface is dry and rugged, covered with *craters* caused by the impact of numerous *meteorites*; this makes it resemble the Moon. Numerous faults, formed during the cooling of the planet when it was young, are also visible on the surface. Constantly baked by its neighbor, the Sun, Mercury has an average surface temperature of 333° F (167° C).

310 miles (500 km)

A Scar-Covered Surface

CALORIS CRATER

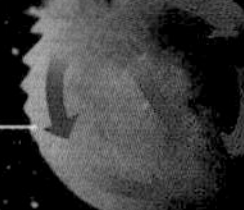

The crater was flooded with lava.

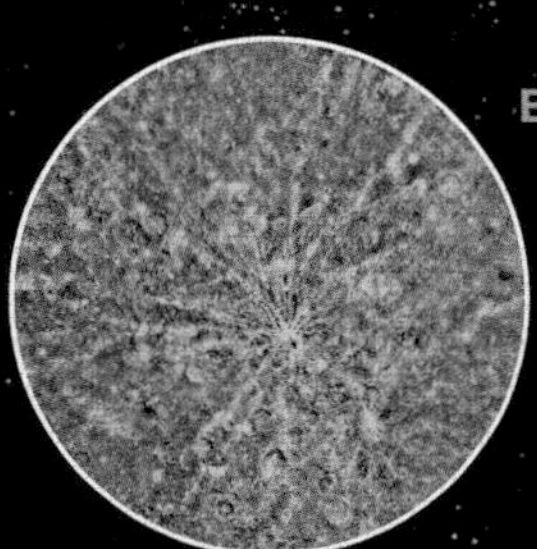

BEETHOVEN

Missions to Mercury

Mariner 10

Messenger

Composition and Magnetic Field

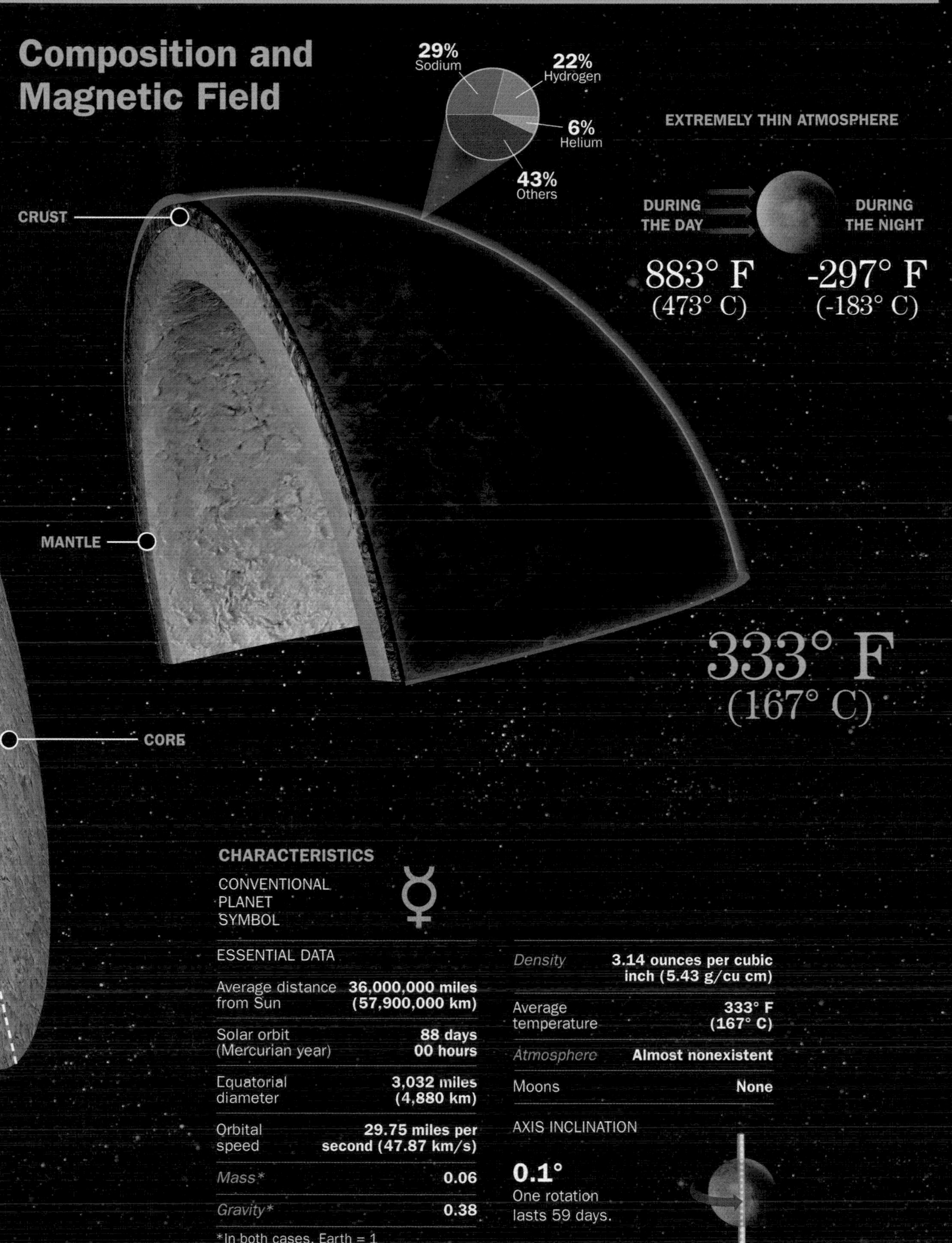
29%
Sodium
22%
Hydrogen
6%
Helium
43%
Others
EXTREMELY THIN ATMOSPHERE
DURING THE DAY
DURING THE NIGHT
883° F
(473° C)
-297° F
(-183° C)
CRUST
MANTLE
CORE
333° F
(167° C)

CHARACTERISTICS

CONVENTIONAL PLANET SYMBOL ☿

ESSENTIAL DATA	
Average distance from Sun	**36,000,000 miles (57,900,000 km)**
Solar orbit (Mercurian year)	**88 days 00 hours**
Equatorial diameter	**3,032 miles (4,880 km)**
Orbital speed	**29.75 miles per second (47.87 km/s)**
*Mass**	**0.06**
*Gravity**	**0.38**

*In both cases, Earth = 1

Density	**3.14 ounces per cubic inch (5.43 g/cu cm)**
Average temperature	**333° F (167° C)**
Atmosphere	**Almost nonexistent**
Moons	**None**

AXIS INCLINATION

0.1°
One rotation lasts 59 days.

Venus, Our Neighbor

Venus is the second closest planet to the Sun. Similar in size to the Earth, it has a volcanic surface, as well as a hostile *atmosphere* governed by the effects of carbon dioxide. Although about four billion years ago the atmospheres of the Earth and Venus were similar, the mass of Venus's atmosphere today is 100 times greater than the Earth's. Its thick clouds of sulfuric acid and dust are so dense that stars are invisible from the planet's surface. Viewed from the Earth, Venus can be bright enough to be visible during day and second only to the moon in brightness at night. Because of this, the movements of Venus were well-known by most ancient civilizations.

CHARACTERISTICS

CONVENTIONAL PLANET SYMBOL ♀

ESSENTIAL DATA

Average distance from the Sun	**67,000,000 miles (108,000,000 km)**
Solar Orbit (Venusian year)	**224 days 17 hours**
Equatorial Diameter	**7,520 miles (12,100 km)**
Orbital speed	**22 miles per second (35 km/s)**
*Mass**	**0.8**
*Gravity**	**0.9**
Density	**3.03 ounces per cubic inch (5.25 g/cu cm)**
Average temperature	**860° F (460° C)**
Atmosphere	**Very thick**
Moons	**None**

*In both cases, Earth = 1

AXIS INCLINATION

117°
Rotates on its own axis every 243 days

Composition

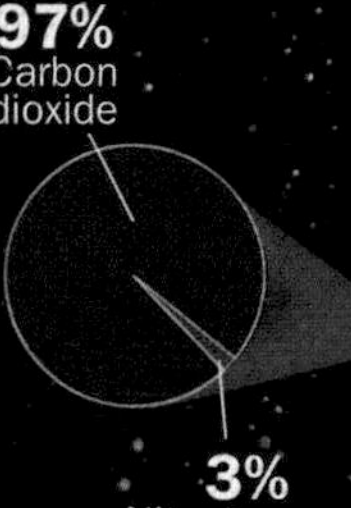
ATMOSPHERE
97%
Carbon dioxide
3%
Nitrogen and traces of other gases

50 miles
(80 km)
IS THE THICKNESS OF THE ATMOSPHERE

CORE
14,400° F
(8,000° C)

MANTLE

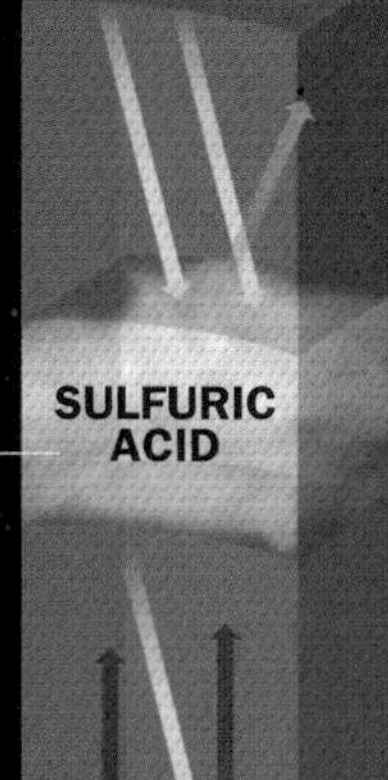
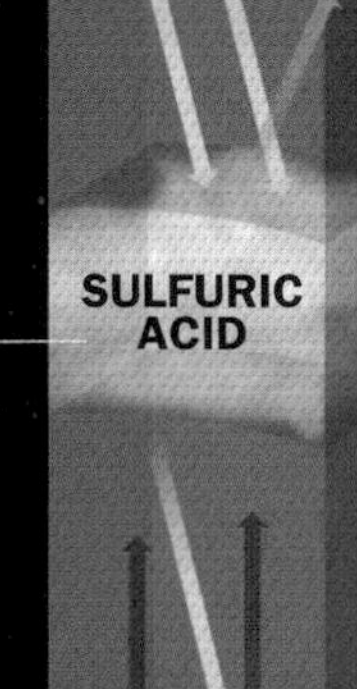
SULFURIC ACID

SOLAR RADIATION

864° F
(462° C)

INFRARED RAYS

VENUS'S PHASES

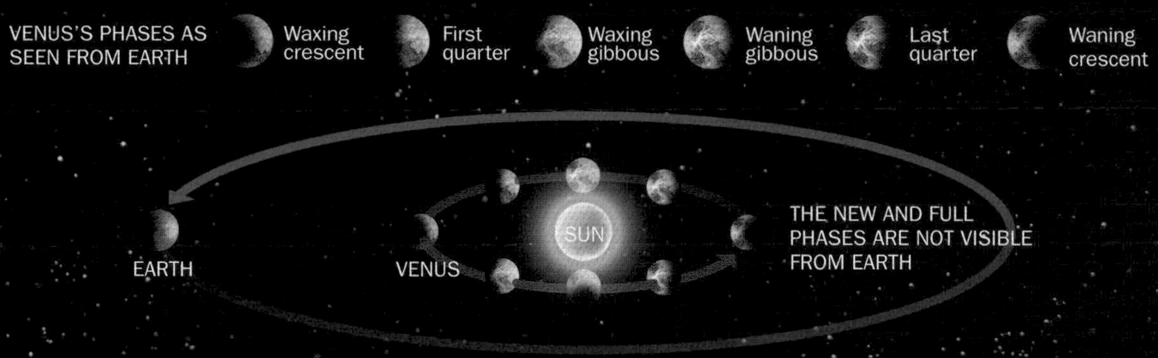

VENUS'S PHASES AS SEEN FROM EARTH

Waxing crescent

First quarter

Waxing gibbous

Waning gibbous

Last quarter

Waning crescent

EARTH

VENUS

SUN

THE NEW AND FULL PHASES ARE NOT VISIBLE FROM EARTH

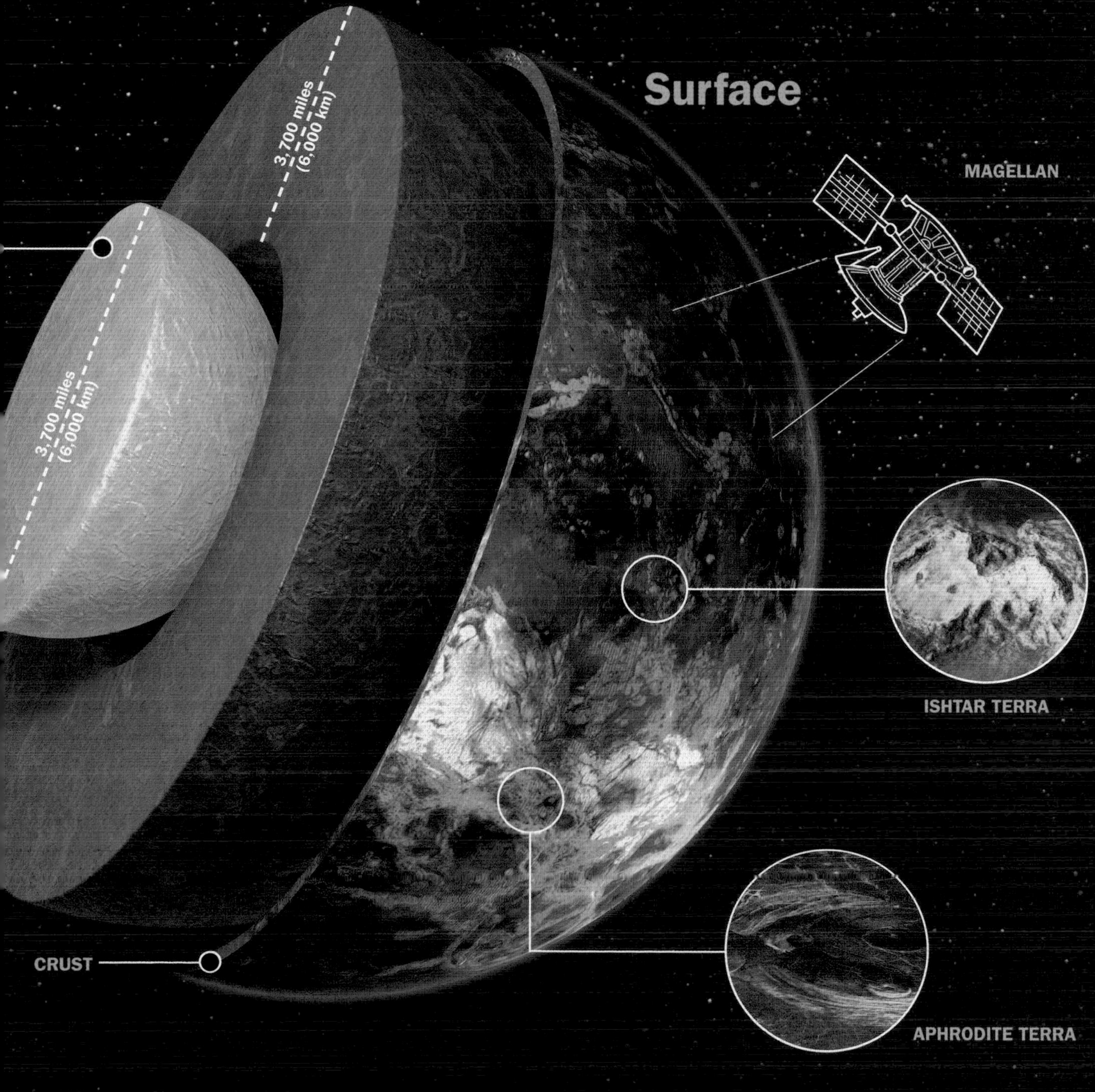

Surface

3,700 miles (6,000 km)

3,700 miles (6,000 km)

MAGELLAN

ISHTAR TERRA

CRUST

APHRODITE TERRA

The Blue Planet

The Earth is known as the blue planet because of the color of the oceans that cover two thirds of its surface. This planet, the third planet from the Sun, is the only one where the right conditions exist to sustain life, something that makes the Earth special. It has liquid water in abundance, a mild temperature, and an atmosphere that protects it from objects that fall from outer space. The *atmosphere* also filters solar radiation thanks to its ozone layer. Slightly flattened at its poles and wider at its equator, the Earth takes 24 hours to revolve once on its axis.

The Phenomenon of Life

70%
WATER

Below 32° F (0° C)	32° F to 212° F (0° C to 100° C)	Above 212° F (100° C)
ONLY ICE	3 STATES	ONLY STEAM

1 EVAPORATION

EARTH MOVEMENTS

SUN

93,500,000 miles (149,503,000 km)

MOON

ROTATION

REVOLUTION

SOUTH POLE

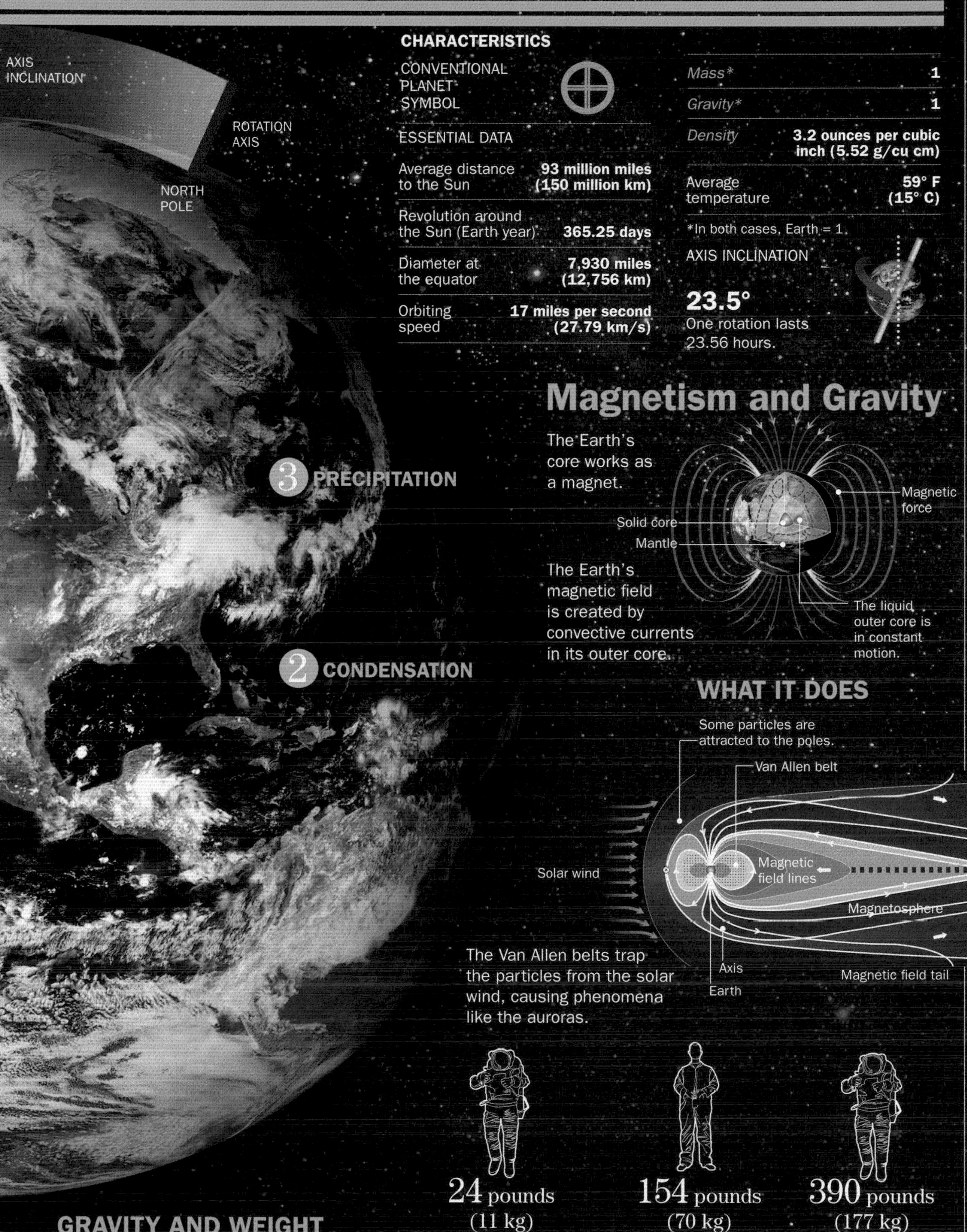
AXIS INCLINATION
ROTATION AXIS
NORTH POLE
3 PRECIPITATION
2 CONDENSATION
CHARACTERISTICS
CONVENTIONAL PLANET SYMBOL
ESSENTIAL DATA
Average distance to the Sun 93 million miles (150 million km)
Revolution around the Sun (Earth year) 365.25 days
Diameter at the equator 7,930 miles (12,756 km)
Orbiting speed 17 miles per second (27.79 km/s)
Mass* 1
Gravity* 1
Density 3.2 ounces per cubic inch (5.52 g/cu cm)
Average temperature 59° F (15° C)
*In both cases, Earth = 1.
AXIS INCLINATION
23.5°
One rotation lasts 23.56 hours.
Magnetism and Gravity
The Earth's core works as a magnet.
Magnetic force
Solid core
Mantle
The Earth's magnetic field is created by convective currents in its outer core.
The liquid outer core is in constant motion.
WHAT IT DOES
Some particles are attracted to the poles.
Van Allen belt
Solar wind
Magnetic field lines
Magnetosphere
Axis
Earth
Magnetic field tail
The Van Allen belts trap the particles from the solar wind, causing phenomena like the auroras.
GRAVITY AND WEIGHT
24 pounds (11 kg) ON THE MOON
154 pounds (70 kg) ON EARTH
390 pounds (177 kg) ON JUPITER

Movements and Coordinates

The Earth rotates on its axis while simultaneously orbiting the Sun. The natural phenomena of night and day, seasons, and years are caused by these movements. To track the passage of time, calendars, clocks, and time zones were invented. Time zones are divided by meridians and assigned a reference hour according to their location. When traveling east, an hour is added with each time zone. An hour is subtracted during westbound travel.

The Earth's Movements

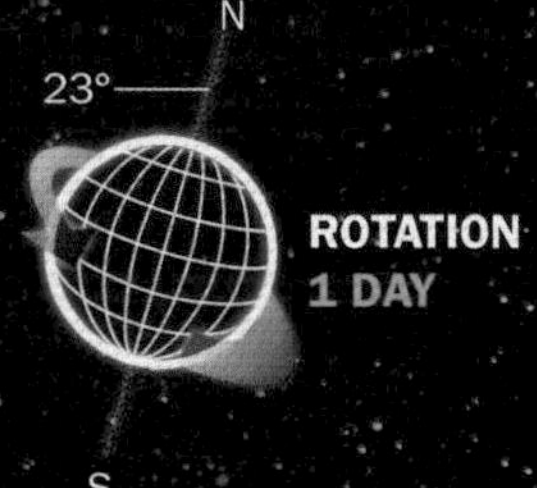
N
23°
S

ROTATION
1 DAY

REVOLUTION
1 YEAR

3°

NUTATION
18.6 YEARS

47°

PRECESSION
25,800 YEARS

June 20 or 21

Summer solstice in the Northern Hemisphere and winter solstice in the Southern Hemisphere.

March 20 or 21

Spring equinox in the Northern Hemisphere and autumn equinox in the Southern Hemisphere.

SUN

September 21 or 22

Autumn equinox in the Northern Hemisphere and spring equinox in the Southern Hemisphere.

23.5°
TILT OF THE EARTH'S AXIS

93 million miles
(149 million km)

THE EARTH'S ORBIT
About 365 days

1 day THE DAYS

About 30 days THE MONTHS

December 20 or 21

Winter solstice in the Northern Hemisphere and summer solstice in the Southern Hemisphere.

Geographic Coordinates

0° GREENWICH MERIDIAN
Northern Hemisphere
PARALLELS
Temperate zone
66.5° N Arctic Circle
23.5° N Tropic of Cancer
0° Equator
Tropical zone
23.5° S Tropic of Capricorn
Polar zone
66.5° S Antarctic Circle
Southern Hemisphere

12:00 A.M.
WEST
EAST
3:00 A.M.
9:00 P.M.
6:00 A.M.
6:00 P.M.
9:00 A.M.
3:00 P.M.
12:00 P.M.

Time Zones

JET LAG

12:00 A.M. Departure time
Northern Hemisphere
12:00 P.M. Arrival time

12:00 15:00 18:00 21:00 0:00 3:00 6:00 9:00

The Moon and Tides

Romance and terror, mystery and superstition–all these emotions are responses to the Moon, the Earth's one natural *satellite*, which always hides one of its two faces. However, whatever symbolic meanings are attributed to the Moon, its *gravitational* pull has a concrete effect on the Earth—it is a cause of the tides. Depending on the distance of the Moon from the Earth, the gravitational pull exerted by the Moon varies in strength and so can high tides and low *tides*. To reach full height, tides need large open areas of ocean. For this reason, tides in closed or small bodies of water are much lower.

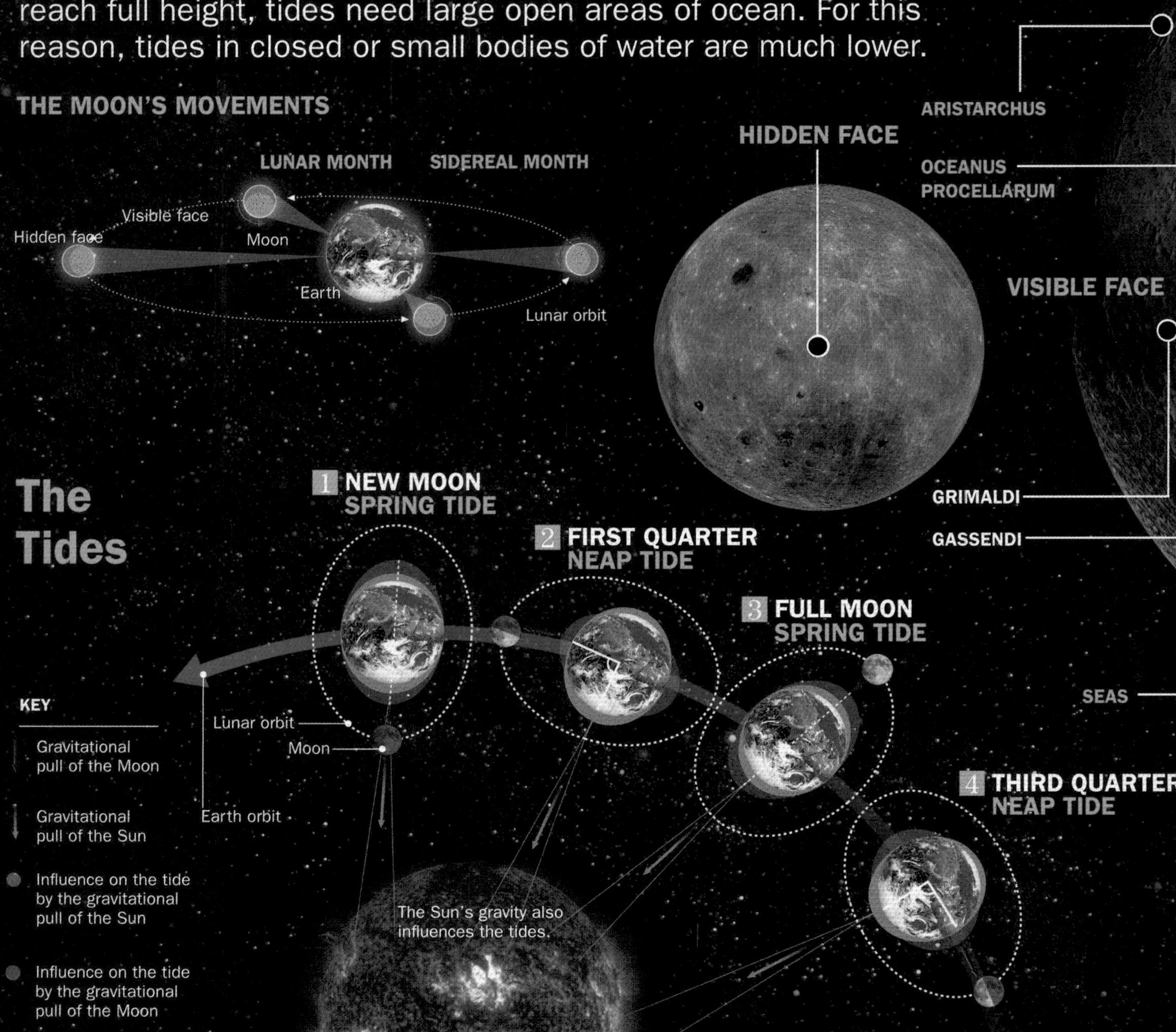

ORIGIN OF THE MOON
THE MOON'S MOVEMENTS
LUNAR MONTH
SIDEREAL MONTH
Visible face
Hidden face
Moon
Earth
Lunar orbit
HIDDEN FACE
ARISTARCHUS
OCEANUS PROCELLARUM
VISIBLE FACE
GRIMALDI
GASSENDI
SEAS
The Tides
1 NEW MOON SPRING TIDE
2 FIRST QUARTER NEAP TIDE
3 FULL MOON SPRING TIDE
4 THIRD QUARTER NEAP TIDE
KEY
Gravitational pull of the Moon
Gravitational pull of the Sun
Influence on the tide by the gravitational pull of the Sun
Influence on the tide by the gravitational pull of the Moon
Lunar orbit
Moon
Earth orbit
The Sun's gravity also influences the tides.

INNER STRUCTURE

ROCKY MANTLE

1000 km

OUTER CORE

100 km

INNER CORE

Mare Imbrium is 3.85 billion years old.

Mare **Nubium**

Mare **Morum**

SCHIKARD TYCHO MAGUINUS

CHARACTERISTICS

CONVENTIONAL SYMBOL

ESSENTIAL DATA	
Average distance from the Earth	**226,400 miles (364,400 km)**
Revolution around the Earth	**27.3 days**
Diameter at the equator	**2,160 miles (3,476 km)**
Orbital speed	**0.6 miles per second (1.02 km/s)**
*Mass**	**0.01**
*Gravity**	**0.17**
Density	**2 ounces per cubic inch (3.34 g/cu cm)**
Temperature	**302° F (150° C) (day) -148° F (-100° C) (night)**
Volume*	**0.02**

*In both cases, Earth = 1

AXIS INCLINATION

5.14°
One rotation lasts 27.32 Earth days.

The Lunar Landscape

MONTES APENNIUS

MOUNTAIN RANGES

COPERNICUS

CRATERS

THE PHASES OF THE MOON

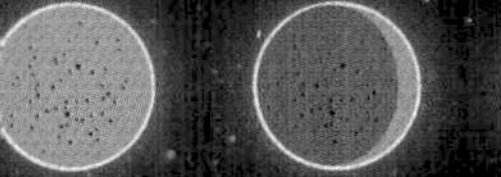

New Moon

Waxing crescent

First quarter

Waxing gibbous

Full Moon

Waning gibbous

Third quarter

Waning crescent

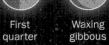

Red and Fascinating

Mars is the fourth planet from the Sun. Of all the planets, Mars most closely resembles the Earth. It has polar ice caps, and the tilt of its axis, period of rotation, and internal structure are similar to those of the Earth. Known as the Red Planet because of the reddish iron oxide that covers its surface, Mars has a thin *atmosphere* composed essentially of carbon dioxide. Mars does not have water, though it did in the past, and there is evidence some water might exist underground. Many spacecraft have been sent to explore Mars, in part because it is the planet other than Earth most likely to have developed some form of life, and it will probably be the first planet humans leave the Earth to visit.

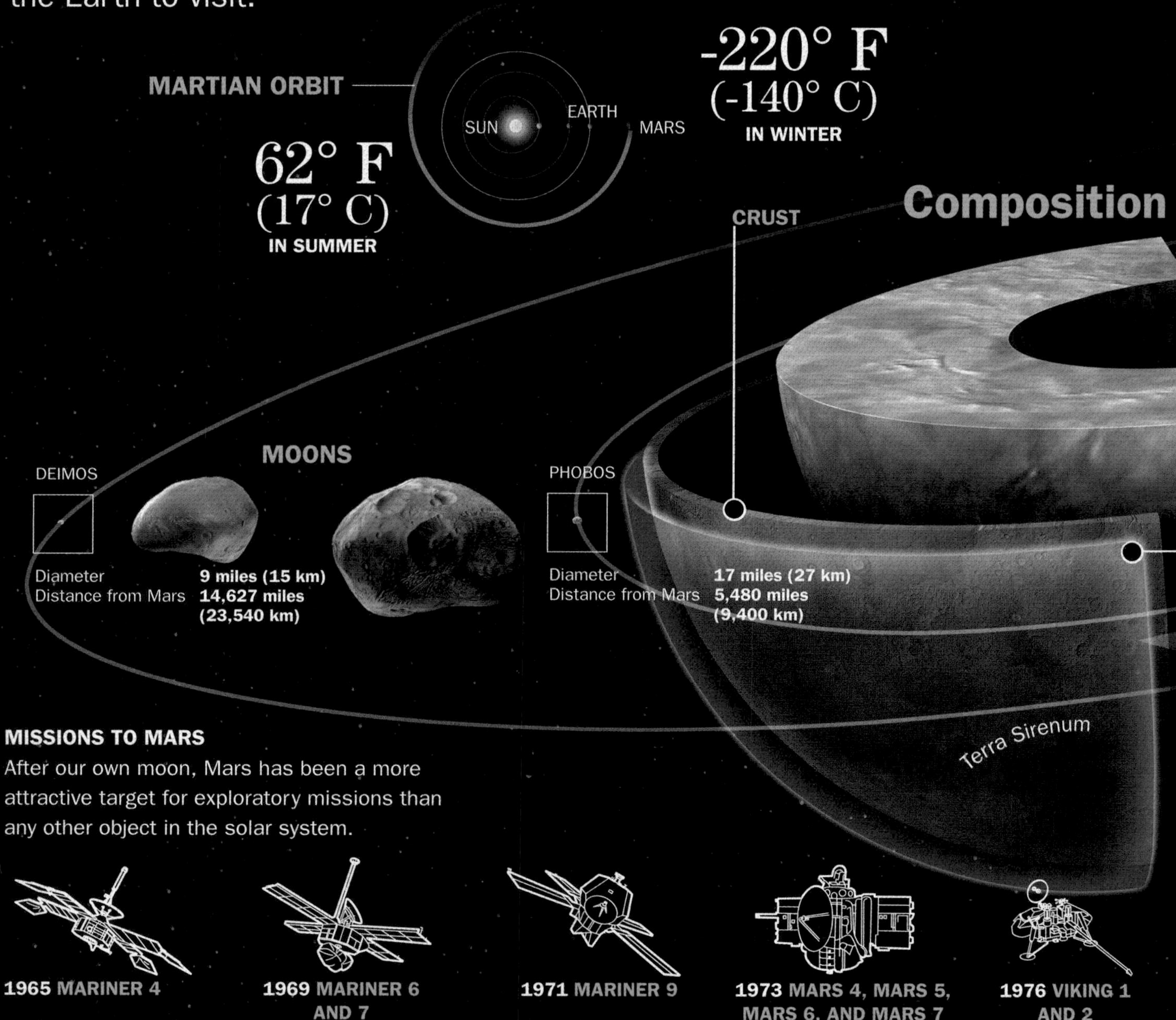

MARTIAN ORBIT
SUN
EARTH
MARS
62° F
(17° C)
IN SUMMER
-220° F
(-140° C)
IN WINTER
Composition
CRUST
MOONS
DEIMOS
Diameter 9 miles (15 km)
Distance from Mars 14,627 miles (23,540 km)
PHOBOS
Diameter 17 miles (27 km)
Distance from Mars 5,480 miles (9,400 km)
Terra Sirenum

MISSIONS TO MARS

After our own moon, Mars has been a more attractive target for exploratory missions than any other object in the solar system.

1965 MARINER 4

1969 MARINER 6 AND 7

1971 MARINER 9

1973 MARS 4, MARS 5, MARS 6, AND MARS 7

1976 VIKING 1 AND 2

Surface

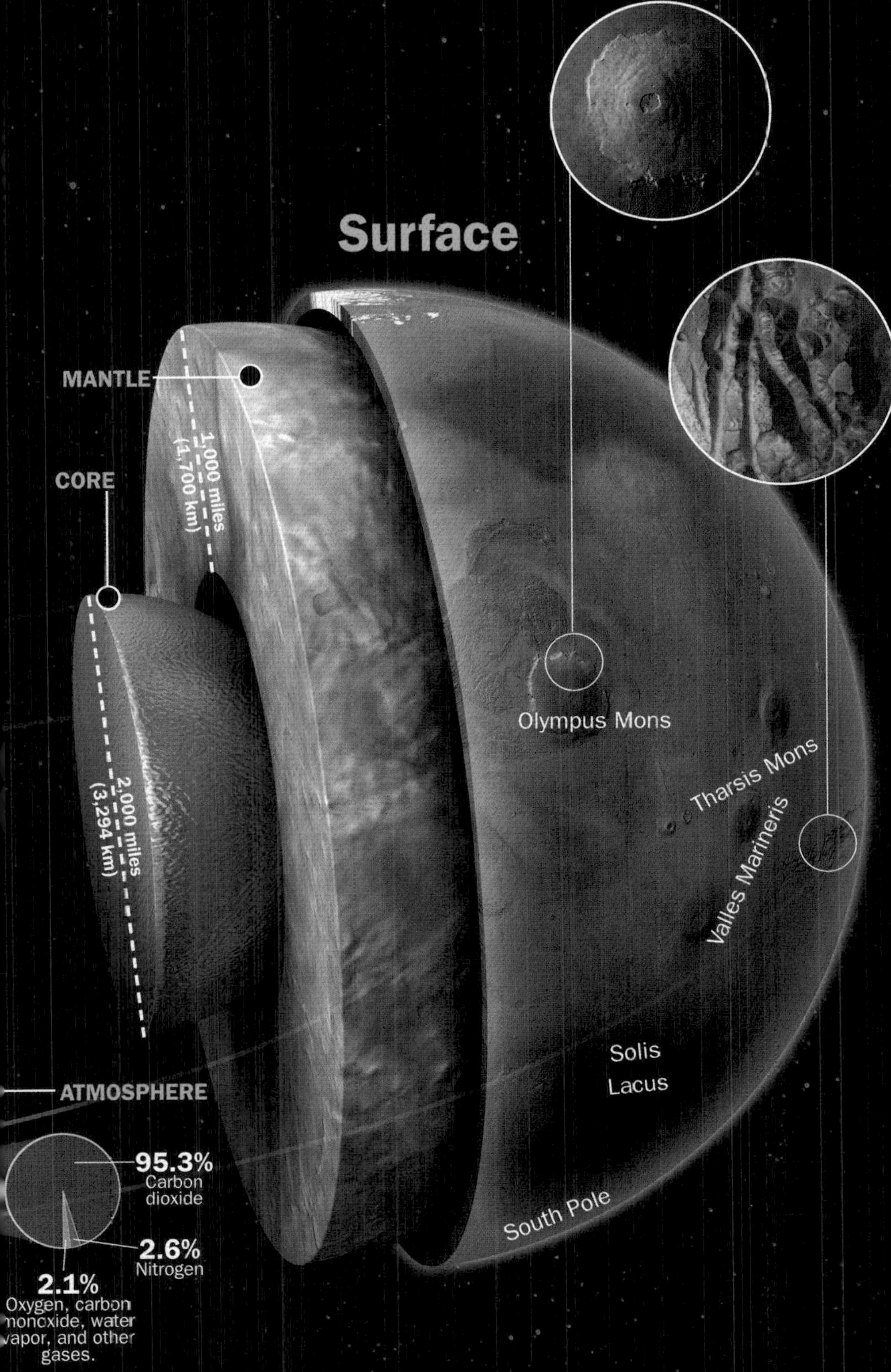

MANTLE
1,000 miles
(1,700 km)
CORE
2,000 miles
(3,294 km)
Olympus Mons
Tharsis Mons
Valles Marineris
Solis
Lacus
South Pole

OLYMPUS MONS

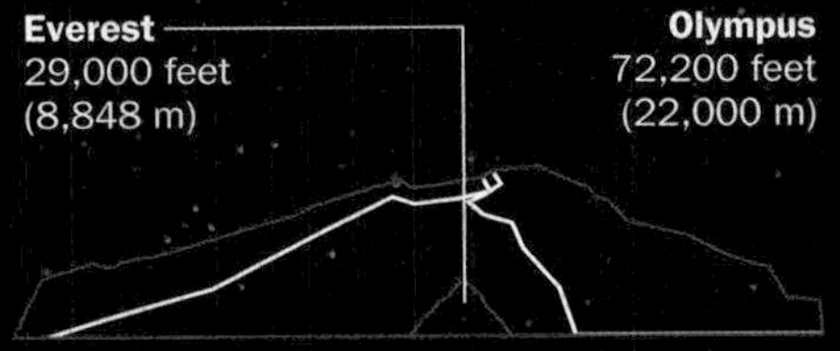

Everest
29,000 feet
(8,848 m)
Olympus
72,200 feet
(22,000 m)

VALLES MARINERIS

CHARACTERISTICS

CONVENTIONAL PLANET SYMBOL

ESSENTIAL DATA	
Average distance from the Sun	**141,600,00 miles (227,900,000 km)**
Solar orbit (Martian year)	**1.88 years**
Equatorial Diameter	**4,222 miles (6,794 km)**
Orbital speed	**15 miles per second (24 km/s)**
*Mass**	**0.107**
*Gravity**	**0.38**
Density	**2.27 ounces per cubic inch (3.93 g/cu cm)**
Average Temperature	**-81° F (-63° C)**
Moons	**2**

*In both cases, Earth = 1

AXIS INCLINATION

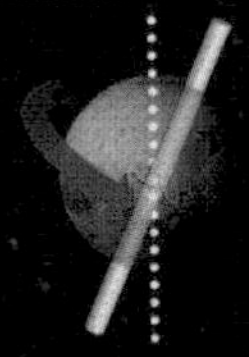

25.2°
One rotation lasts 1.88 years.

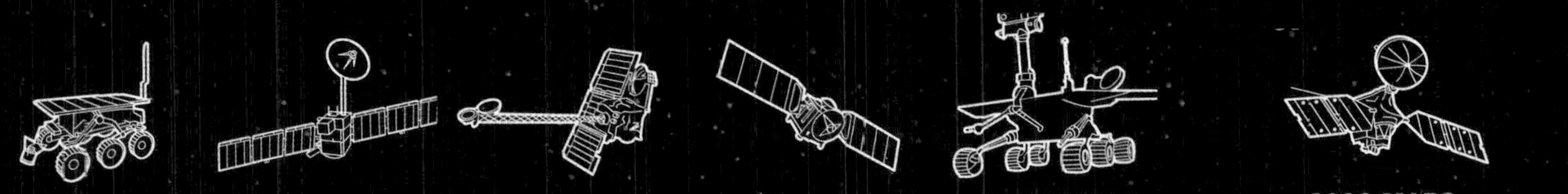

ATMOSPHERE

95.3%
Carbon dioxide
2.6%
Nitrogen
2.1%
Oxygen, carbon monoxide, water vapor, and other gases.

1997 MARS PATHFINDER

1997 MARS GLOBAL SURVEYOR

2001 MARS ODYSSEY

2003 MARS EXPRESS

2004 SPIRIT AND OPPORTUNITY

2006 MARS RECONNAISSANCE ORBITER

Mars in the Sights

There was a time when it was thought that Mars, our closest neighbor, harbored life. Perhaps for this reason it is the planet that has been most explored by various spacecraft from the decade of the 1960s onward, and it is therefore the one we know the best, apart from the Earth. *Mariner 9* in 1971 and *Vikings 1* and *2* in 1976 revealed the existence of valleys and immense volcanic mountains. In 2001 the United States launched the Mars Odyssey mission, which indicated that liquid water exists at great depths.

Mars Odyssey Mission

DISCOVERY

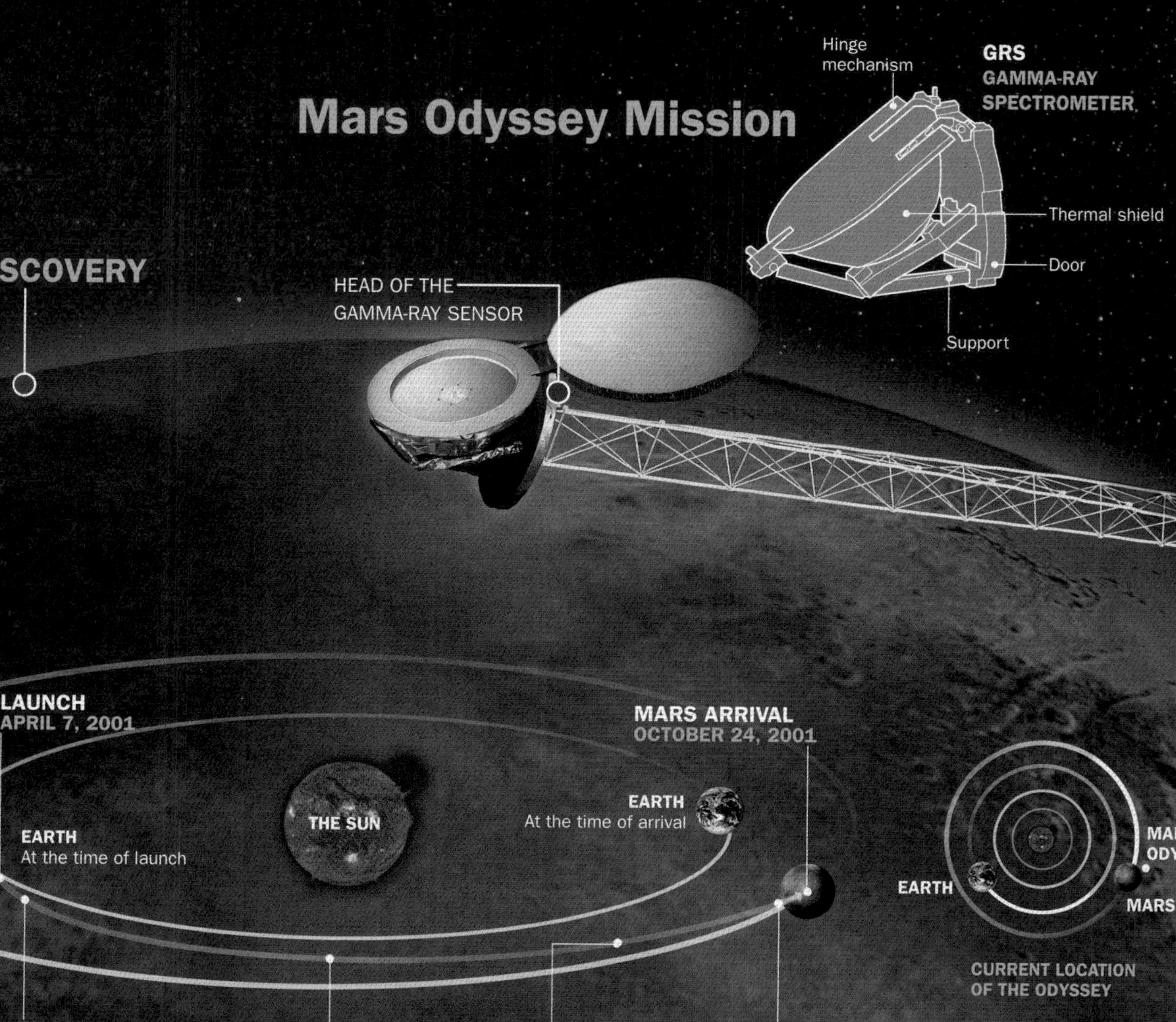

Hinge mechanism
GRS
GAMMA-RAY SPECTROMETER
Thermal shield
Door
Support
HEAD OF THE GAMMA-RAY SENSOR
LAUNCH
APRIL 7, 2001
MARS ARRIVAL
OCTOBER 24, 2001
EARTH
At the time of launch
THE SUN
EARTH
At the time of arrival
MAY 2001
JUNE 2001
JULY 2001
SEPTEMBER 2001
EARTH
MARS
CURRENT LOCATION OF THE ODYSSEY

TECHNICAL SPECIFICATIONS

Launch	**April 7, 2001**
Arrived on Mars	**October 24, 2001**
Cost of the mission	**$332 million**
Weight	**1,600 pounds (725 kg)**
Useful life	**10 years**

7 feet (2.2 m)

8.5 feet (2.6 m)

Earth Seen from Mars

THE BLUE PLANET

HIGH-GAIN
ANTENNA

SOLAR PANELS

NEUTRON
SPECTROMETER

VIDEOCAMERAS

NEUTRON
ENERGY
DETECTOR

UHF ANTENNA

7 months
THE TIME IT TOOK MARS ODYSSEY TO REACH ITS TARGET

SURFACE OF MARS

THEMIS
THERMAL EMISSION IMAGING SYSTEM

Martian Robots

Spirit and Opportunity, the twin *robots* launched in June 2003 from Earth that landed on Martian soil in January 2004, were designed to travel over the surface of the Red Planet. Both vehicles are part of NASA's Mars Exploration Rovers mission. They have tools that allow them to drill into rock and take samples of the soil to analyze their chemical composition. The robots are located on opposite sides of the planet to explore two uniquely different places. They each use nine cameras.

How It Got to Mars

Aeroshell

1 DECELERATION

Parachutes

2 PARACHUTES

3 FALL

Entry module

4 ROCKETS

5 AIR BAGS

Descent rockets

6 DESTINATION

Vectran air bags

7 INSTRUMENTS

Photograph of the surface taken by Spirit

70,000 images

Obtained by Spirit in its first two years

Track and photograph taken by Opportunity

80,000 images

Obtained by Opportunity in its first two years on Mars

Water and Life on Mars

On this mission, NASA hoped to find evidence of water and life.

TECHNICAL SPECIFICATIONS

Date of landing	**Spirit: January 3, 2004** **Opportunity: January 24, 2004**
Cost of the mission	**$820 million**
Progress per day	**330 feet (100 m)**
Plutonium	**Each spacecraft carries 0.01 ounces (2.8 g)**
Useful life	**More than two years**

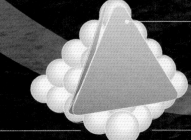

5 feet
(1.5 m)

WEIGHT ON EARTH

384 pounds (174 kg)

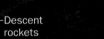

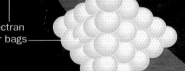

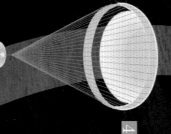

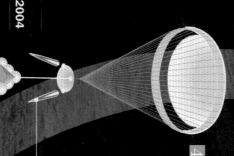

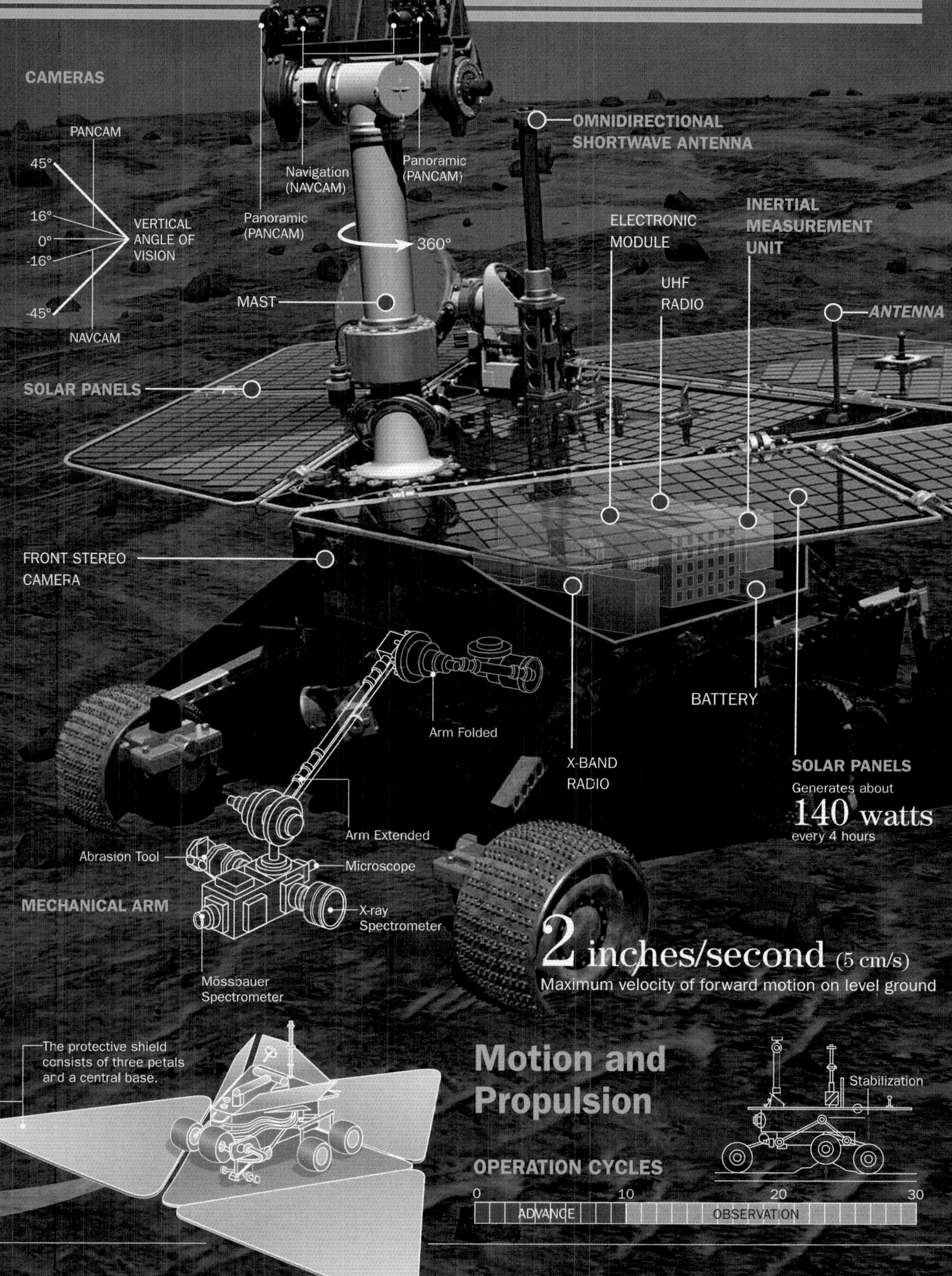
CAMERAS
PANCAM
45°
16°
0°
-16°
-45°
VERTICAL ANGLE OF VISION
NAVCAM
Navigation (NAVCAM)
Panoramic (PANCAM)
Panoramic (PANCAM)
360°
MAST
OMNIDIRECTIONAL SHORTWAVE ANTENNA
ELECTRONIC MODULE
UHF RADIO
INERTIAL MEASUREMENT UNIT
ANTENNA
SOLAR PANELS
FRONT STEREO CAMERA
Arm Folded
Arm Extended
Abrasion Tool
Microscope
MECHANICAL ARM
X-ray Spectrometer
Mössbauer Spectrometer
BATTERY
X-BAND RADIO
SOLAR PANELS
Generates about
140 watts
every 4 hours
2 inches/second (5 cm/s)
Maximum velocity of forward motion on level ground
The protective shield consists of three petals and a central base.
Stabilization
OPERATION CYCLES
0
10
20
30
ADVANCE
OBSERVATION

Motion and Propulsion

Jupiter, Gas Giant

Jupiter is the largest planet in the solar system. Its diameter is 11 times that of the Earth, and its mass is 300 times as great. Because the speed of Jupiter's rotation flattens the planet at its poles, its equatorial diameter is greater than its polar diameter. Jupiter rotates at 25,000 miles per hour (40,000 km/hr). One of the most distinctive elements of Jupiter's *atmosphere* is its so-called Great Red Spot, a giant high-pressure region of turbulence that has been observed from the Earth for more than 300 years.

Composition

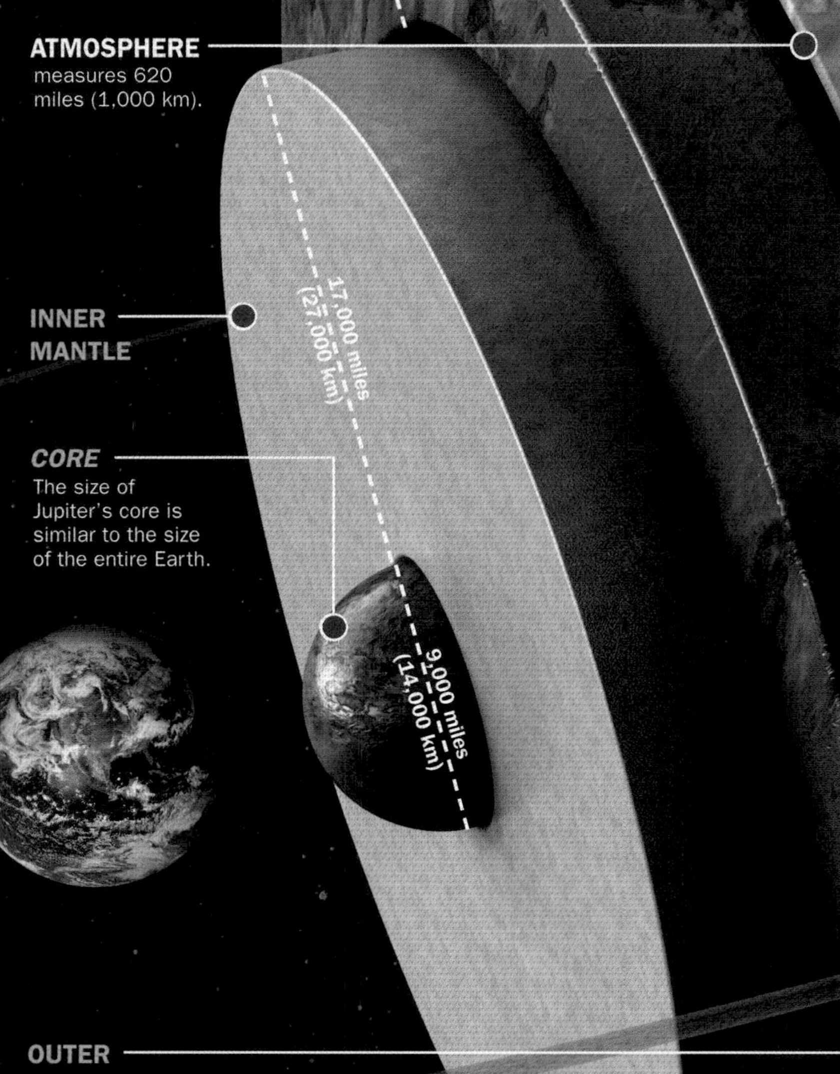

23,000 miles (37,000 km)
ATMOSPHERE measures 620 miles (1,000 km).
INNER MANTLE
17,000 miles (27,000 km)
CORE The size of Jupiter's core is similar to the size of the entire Earth.
9,000 miles (14,000 km)
OUTER MANTLE

CHARACTERISTICS

CONVENTIONAL PLANET SYMBOL ♃

ESSENTIAL DATA	
Average distance from the Sun	**483,000,000 miles (778,000,000 km)**
Solar orbit (Jovian year)	**11 years, 312 days**
Equatorial Diameter	**88,700 miles (142,800 km)**
Orbital speed	**8 miles per second (13 km/s)**
*Mass**	**318**
*Gravity**	**2.36**
Density	**0.77 ounces per cubic inch (1.33 g/cu cm)**
Average Temperature	**-184° F (-120° C)**
Atmosphere	**Very dense**
Moons	**More than 60**

*In both cases, Earth = 1

AXIS INCLINATION

3.1°

One rotation 9 hours and 55 minutes.

The Moons of Jupiter

Europa
2,000 miles
(3,200 km)

Io
2,264 miles
(3,643 km)

Ganymede
3,270 miles
(5,268 km)

Callisto
2,986 miles
(4,806 km)

GALILEAN MOONS

Winds

16,160 miles
(26,000 km)
GREAT RED SPOT

RING MATERIAL

RINGS

OUTER GOSSAMER RING

INNER GOSSAMER RING

MAIN RING

HALO

ATMOSPHERE

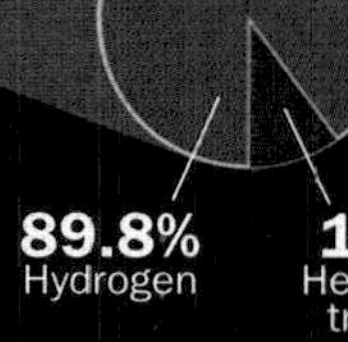
89.8%
Hydrogen
10.2%
Helium with traces of methane and ammonia

JUPITER'S MAGNETISM

400,000,000 miles
(650,000,0000° C)

Jupiter in Focus

The fifth planet of the solar system was visited by Pioneer 1 and 2, Voyager 1 and 2, and Cassini. However, the most significant visitor was Galileo, launched by NASA on Oct. 18, 1989. Galileo consisted of an orbiter and an atmospheric *probe*. After a long voyage, the atmospheric probe penetrated some 125 miles (200 km) into the *atmosphere* of Jupiter on Dec. 7, 1995, transmitting data about the atmosphere's chemical composition and Jupiter's meteorological activity. The orbiter continued sending information until it crashed into the gaseous giant on Sept. 21, 2003.

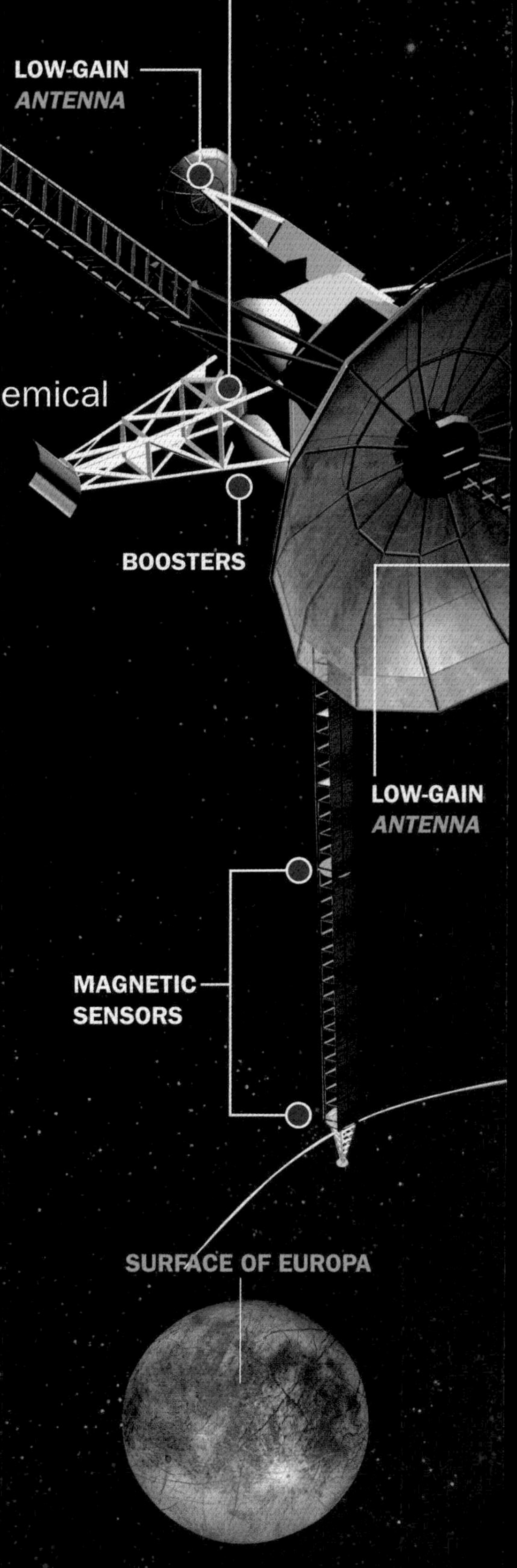

ATMOSPHERIC PROBE

LOW-GAIN *ANTENNA*

BOOSTERS

LOW-GAIN *ANTENNA*

MAGNETIC SENSORS

SURFACE OF EUROPA

Trajectory

14 years was the duration of the Galileo mission—from October 1989 to September 2003.

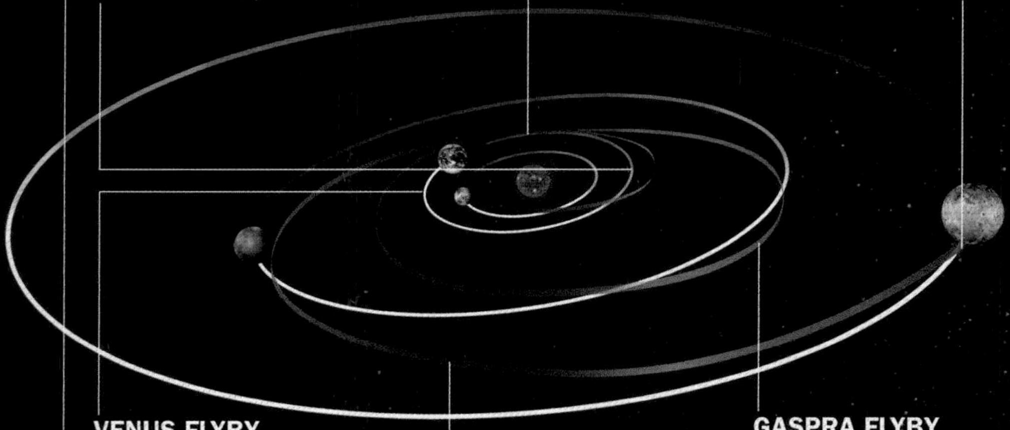

LAUNCH
OCTOBER 18, 1989

EARTH FLYBYS
DECEMBER 1990/ AUGUST 1992

ARRIVAL AT JUPITER
DECEMBER 7, 1995

VENUS FLYBY
FEBRUARY 10, 1990

IDA FLYBY
AUGUST 28, 1993

GASPRA FLYBY
OCTOBER 29, 1991

Atmospheric Probe

DESCENT INTO JUPITER

1 RELEASE

2 SHIELDING

3 PARACHUTE

Deceleration module

Antenna

Parachutes

Descent module

4 DESCENT

Parachutes

Galileo

TECHNICAL SPECIFICATIONS

Date of arrival	**December 7, 1995**
Cost of the mission	**$1.5 billion**
Useful life	**14 years**
Weight without the probe	**4,900 pounds (2,223 kg)**
Organization	**NASA**

23 feet (7 m)

20 feet (6.2 m)

ATMOSPHERE OF JUPITER

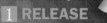

IO

TECHNICAL SPECIFICATIONS

Entry into the atmosphere	**December 7, 1995**
Active life	**57 minutes**
Weight	**750 pounds (339 kg)**
Organization	**NASA**

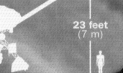

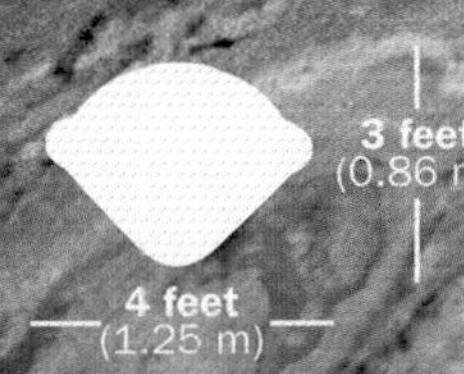

3 feet (0.86 m)

4 feet (1.25 m)

The Lord of the Rings

Saturn is the solar system's second largest planet. Like Jupiter, it is a large ball of gas surrounding a small, solid *core*. Saturn was the most distant planet discovered before the invention of the *telescope*. To the naked eye, it looks like a yellowish star, but with the help of a telescope, its rings are clearly visible. Ten times farther from the Sun than the Earth, Saturn is the least dense planet. If an ocean could be found large enough to hold it, Saturn would float.

Rings

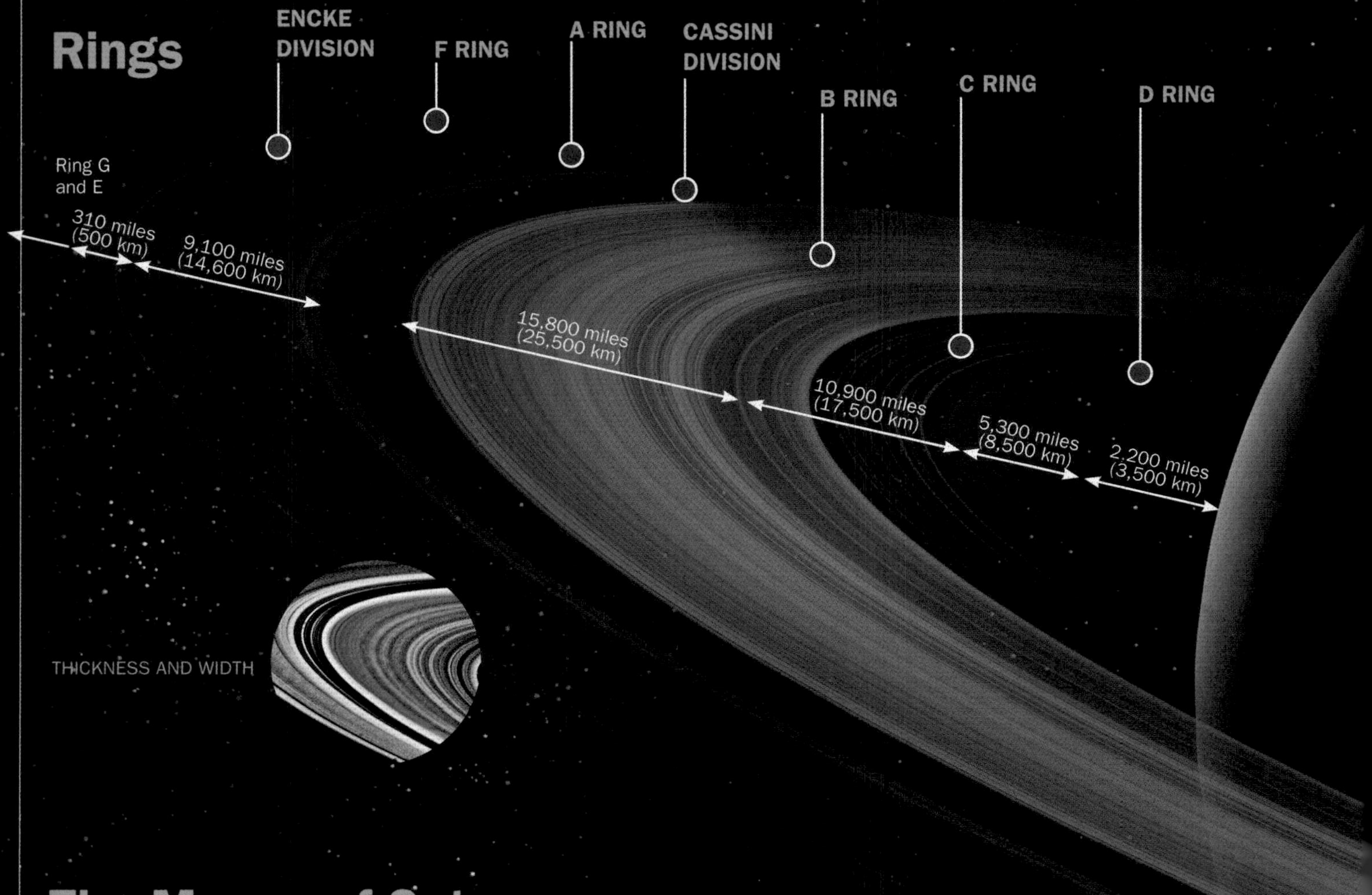

ENCKE DIVISION

F RING

A RING

CASSINI DIVISION

B RING

C RING

D RING

Ring G and E

310 miles (500 km)

9,100 miles (14,600 km)

15,800 miles (25,500 km)

10,900 miles (17,500 km)

5,300 miles (8,500 km)

2,200 miles (3,500 km)

THICKNESS AND WIDTH

The Moons of Saturn

Titan's diameter is larger than Mercury's. It has an *atmosphere* that is mostly made of nitrogen.

Surface

HAZE

WHITE CLOUDS

DEEP AND ORANGE CLOUDS

BLUISH CLOUDS

WINDS

Gaseous Exterior

COMPONENTS

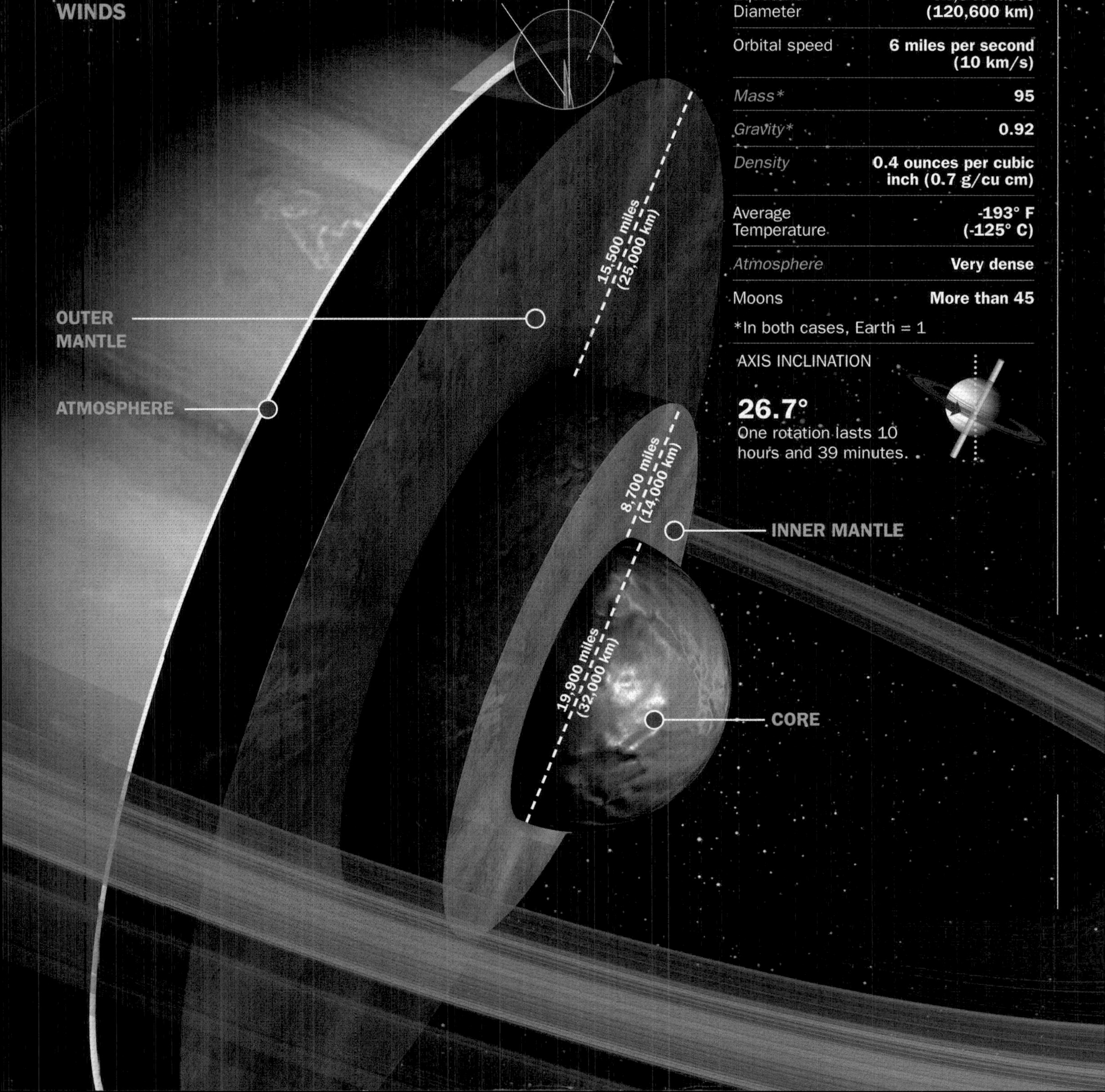

<1% Sulfur gives it a yellowish appearance

2% Helium

97% Hydrogen

OUTER MANTLE

ATMOSPHERE

15,500 miles (25,000 km)

8,700 miles (14,000 km)

19,900 miles (32,000 km)

INNER MANTLE

CORE

CHARACTERISTICS

CONVENTIONAL PLANET SYMBOL ♄

ESSENTIAL DATA	
Average distance from the Sun	**887,000,000 miles (1,427,000,000 km)**
Solar orbit (Saturnine year)	**29 years 154 days**
Equatorial Diameter	**74,940 miles (120,600 km)**
Orbital speed	**6 miles per second (10 km/s)**
*Mass**	**95**
*Gravity**	**0.92**
Density	**0.4 ounces per cubic inch (0.7 g/cu cm)**
Average Temperature	**-193° F (-125° C)**
Atmosphere	**Very dense**
Moons	**More than 45**

*In both cases, Earth = 1

AXIS INCLINATION

26.7°
One rotation lasts 10 hours and 39 minutes.

A View of Saturn

The longed-for return to Saturn was the result of a scientific alliance between NASA and the European Space Agency (ESA). On Oct. 15, 1997, after a number of years of development, the fruit of this collaboration lifted off toward this enormous gas giant. The mission of Cassini, the mother ship, was the exploration of Saturn. It carried a smaller *probe*, Huygens, that was to land on Saturn's largest moon, Titan, and transmit images and sounds from the surface. The Huygens probe accomplished this feat, demonstrating once again the capacity of humans to respond to the challenge of frontiers.

Trajectory

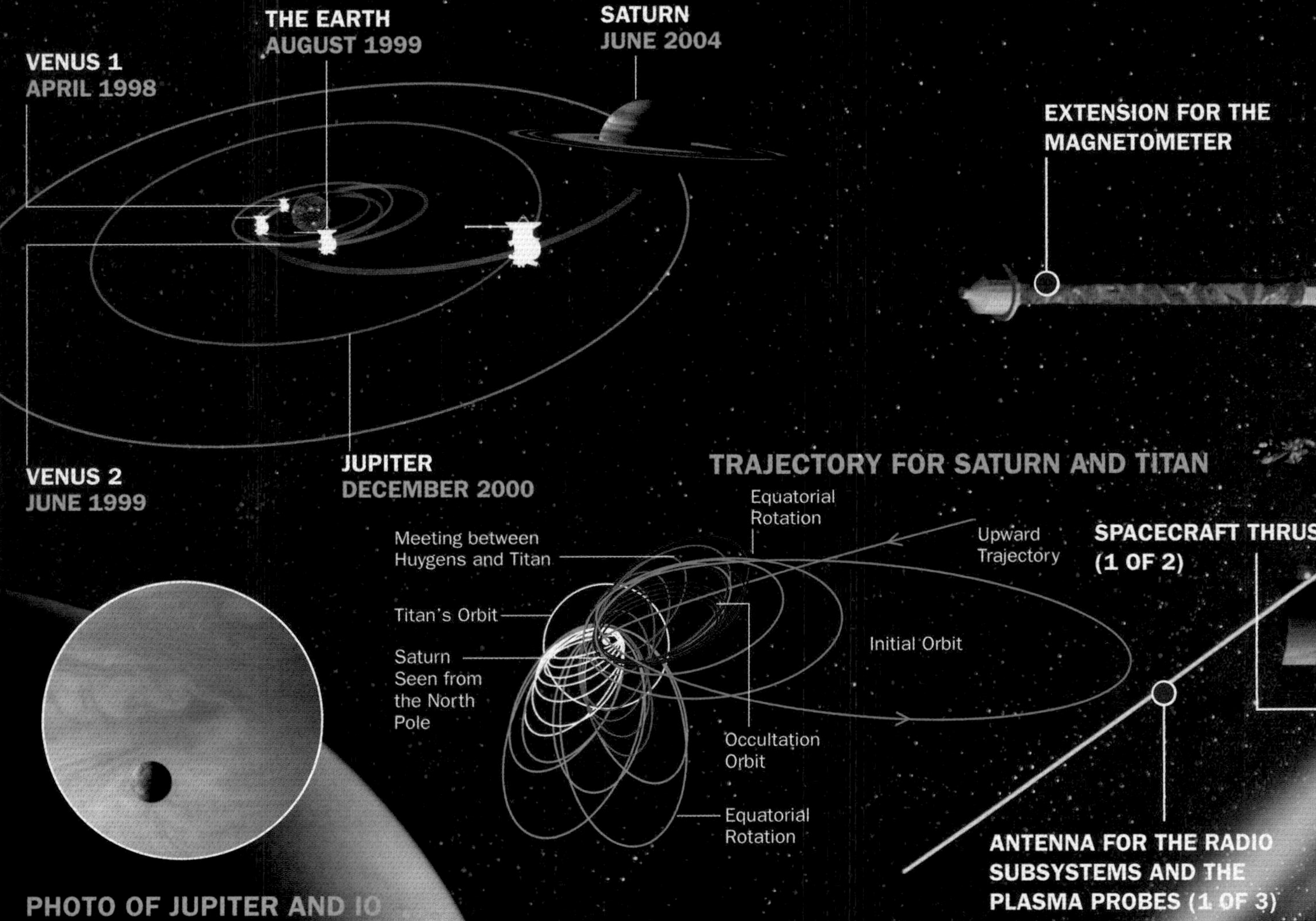
VENUS 1
APRIL 1998
THE EARTH
AUGUST 1999
SATURN
JUNE 2004
VENUS 2
JUNE 1999
JUPITER
DECEMBER 2000
TRAJECTORY FOR SATURN AND TITAN
Equatorial Rotation
Meeting between Huygens and Titan
Upward Trajectory
Titan's Orbit
Initial Orbit
Saturn Seen from the North Pole
Occultation Orbit
Equatorial Rotation

PHOTO OF JUPITER AND IO

THE RINGS OF SATURN

EXTENSION FOR THE MAGNETOMETER

SPACECRAFT THRUSTE (1 OF 2)

ANTENNA FOR THE RADIO SUBSYSTEMS AND THE PLASMA PROBES (1 OF 3)

Cassini-Huygens

TECHNICAL SPECIFICATIONS

Date of launch	**October 15, 1997**
Begins Saturn orbit	**July 1, 2004**
Closest approach	**11,800 miles (19,000 km)**
Weight	**12,300 pounds (5,600 kg)**
Organizations	**NASA and ESA**

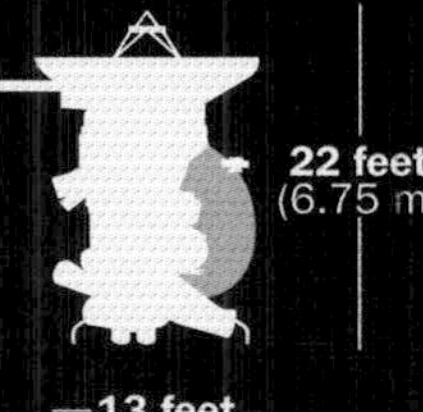
22 feet
(6.75 m)
13 feet
(4 m)

12,300 pounds (5,600 kg)

WEIGHT ON EARTH

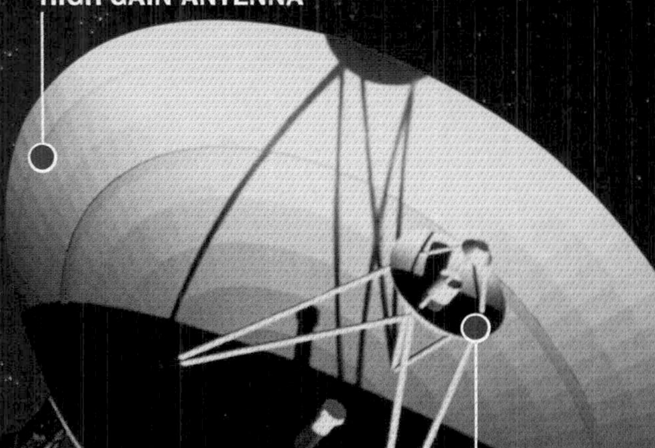
HIGH-GAIN ANTENNA
LOW-GAIN ANTENNA (1 OF 2)
RADAR
TELESCOPES
RTG (RADIOISOTOPE THERMOELECTRIC GENERATOR)

Descent onto Titan

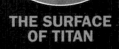

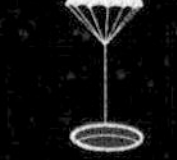

1 SEPARATION
2 DESCENT
3 FIRST PARACHUTE
4 SECOND PARACHUTE
5 THIRD PARACHUTE
6 DEPLOYS ITS LANDING FEET
7 IMPACT ON THE SURFACE
8 LANDING
THE SURFACE OF TITAN

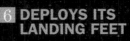

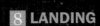

TECHNICAL SPECIFICATIONS: HUYGENS

Date of release	**December 25, 2004**
Weight	**703 pounds (39 kg)**
Organizations	**NASA and ESA**
Data of landing	**January 14, 2005**
Descent by parachute	**2.5 hours**

Uranus Without Secrets

To the unaided eye, Uranus looks like a star at the limit of visibility. It is the seventh farthest planet from the Sun and the third largest planet in the solar system. One peculiarity distinguishing it from the other planets is its anomalous axis of rotation, tilted nearly 98 degrees around the plane of its orbit, so that one or the other of Uranus's poles points toward the Sun. Astronomers speculate that, during its formation, Uranus may have suffered an impact with a proto planet, which could have altered Uranus's tilt. Uranus's orbit is so large that the planet takes 84 years to completely orbit the Sun. Uranus's period of rotation is 17 hours and 14 minutes.

CHARACTERISTICS

CONVENTIONAL PLANET SYMBOL	
ESSENTIAL DATA	
Average distance from the Sun	**1,780,000,000 miles (2,870,000,000 km)**
Solar orbit (Uranian year)	**84 years 4 days**
Equatorial Diameter	**32,200 miles (51,800 km)**
Orbital speed	**4 miles per second (7 km/s)**
*Mass**	**14.5**
*Gravity**	**0.89**
Density	**0.8 ounces per cubic inch (1.3 g/cu cm)**
Average Temperature	**-346° F (-210° C)**
Atmosphere	**Less Dense**
Moons	**27**

*In both cases, Earth = 1

AXIS INCLINATION

97.9°

One rotation lasts 17 hours and 14 minutes.

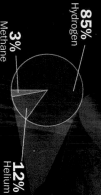

Composition

CORE

INNER MANTLE

OUTER MANTLE

ATMOSPHERE

6,200 miles (10,000 km)

10,600 miles (17,000 km)

6,200 miles (10,000 km)

85% Hydrogen

3% Methane

12% Helium

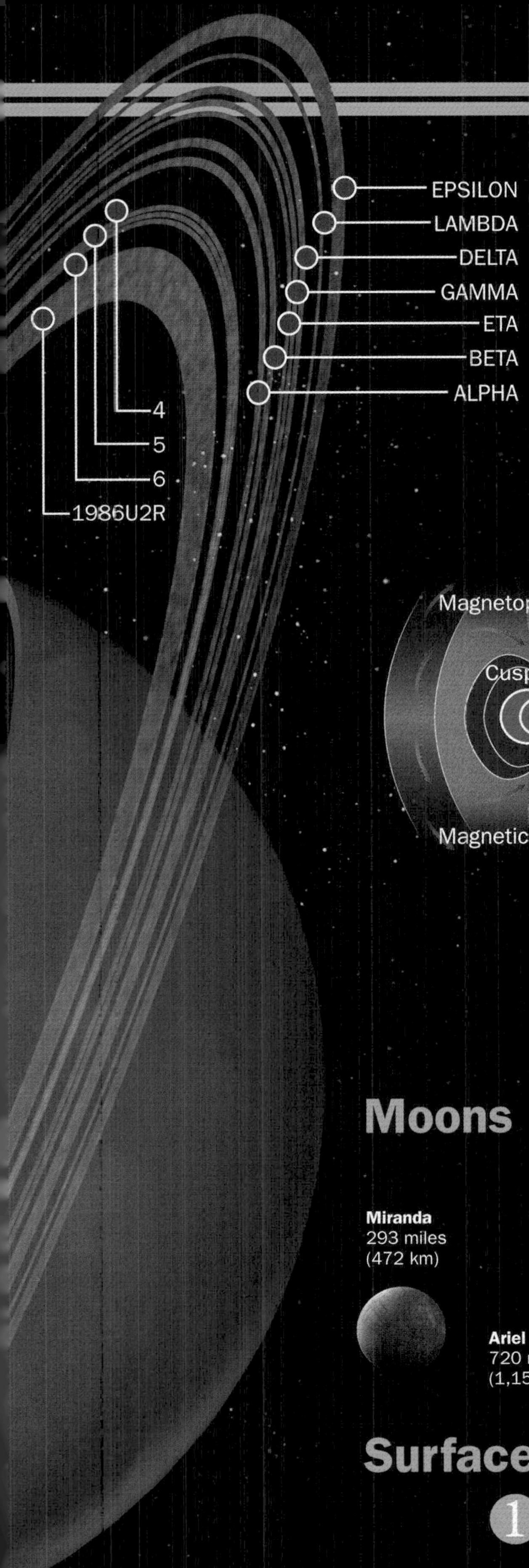

EPSILON
LAMBDA
DELTA
GAMMA
ETA
BETA
ALPHA
4
5
6
1986U2R

Rings

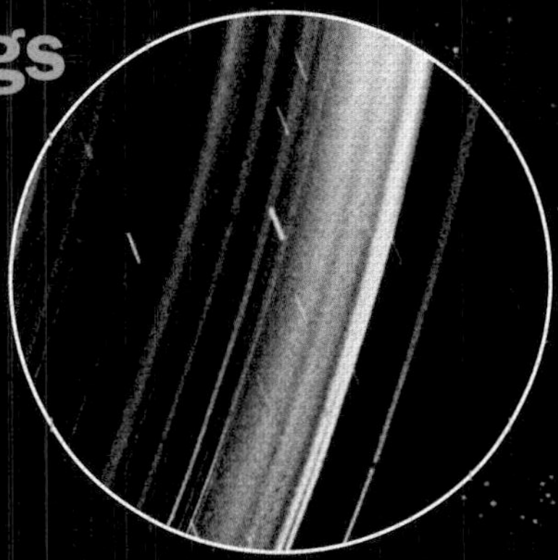

MAGNETIC FIELD

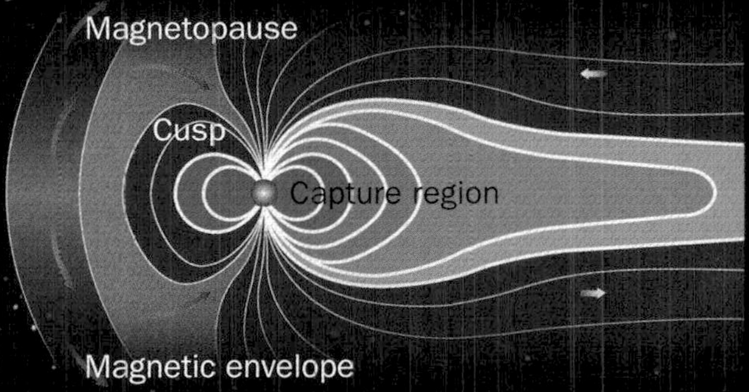

Magnetopause
Cusp
Capture region
Magnetic envelope

Moons

Titania
980 miles
(1,578 km)
Umbriel
730 miles
(1,170 km)
Miranda
293 miles
(472 km)
Ariel
720 miles
(1,158 km)
Oberon
946 miles
(1,522 km)

Surface

REFRACTION OF RAYS

1 REFLECTION

2 METHANE

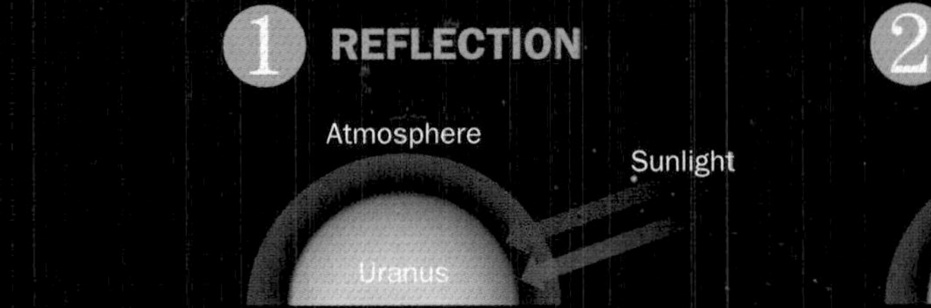
Atmosphere
Sunlight
Uranus
Atmosphere
Sunlight
Uranus

Neptune: Deep Blue

Seen from our planet, Neptune appears as a faint, blue point invisible to the naked eye. Images sent to Earth by *Voyager 2* show the planet as a remarkably blue sphere, an effect produced by the presence of methane in the outer part of Neptune's *atmosphere*. The farthest of the gaseous planets, Neptune is 30 times farther from the Sun than the Earth is. Its rings and impressive clouds are noteworthy, as is its resemblance to Uranus. Neptune is of special interest to astronomers because, before its discovery, its existence and location were predicted on the basis of mathematical calculations.

Moons

TRITON

-391° F
(-235° C)

is its temperature, making Triton one of the coldest bodies in the solar system.

1,200
miles per hour
(2,000 km/h)

Rings

ADAMS
ARAGO
LE VERRIER
LASSELL
GALLE

COMPOSITION

Surface

Ascending winds

Descending winds

THE GREAT SPOT

Hard Heart

8,700 miles (14,000 km)

3,700 miles (6,000 km)

CORE

INNER MANTLE

OUTER MANTLE

ATMOSPHERE

4,500 miles (7,200 km)

89.8% Hydrogen

10.2% Helium

CHARACTERISTICS

CONVENTIONAL PLANET SYMBOL ♆

ESSENTIAL DATA	
Average distance from the Sun	**2,800,000,000 miles (4,500,000,000 km)**
Solar orbit (Neptunian year)	**164 years 264 days**
Equatorial Diameter	**30,800 miles (49,500 km)**
Orbital speed	**3.4 miles per second (5.5 km/s)**
*Mass**	**17.2**
*Gravity**	**1.12**
Density	**1 ouncez per cubic inch (1.6 g/cu cm)**
Average Temperature	**-330° F (-200° C)**
Atmosphere	**Dense**
Moons	**13**

*In both cases, Earth = 1

AXIS INCLINATION

28.3°

One rotation lasts 16 hours and 36 minutes.

The Road Beyond

The space probes Voyager 1 and 2 were launched by NASA to study the outer solar system. Voyager 1 was launched on Sept. 5, 1977, and flew by Jupiter in 1979 and Saturn in 1980. Voyager 2 lifted off on Aug. 20, 1977, then flew by Jupiter and Saturn to reach Uranus in 1986 and Neptune in 1989. Voyager 2 is the only probe that has visited both of these planets. Both probes have now become the furthest distant artificial instruments ever sent into space by humans.

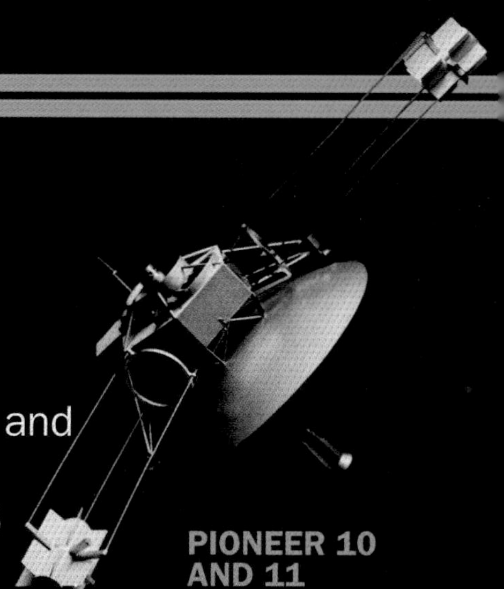

PIONEER 10 AND 11

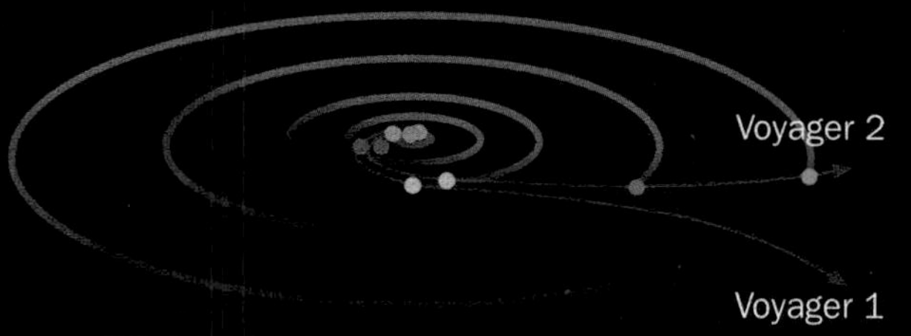

Voyager 2
Voyager 1
TRAJECTORY
EARTH
JUPITER
SATURN
URANUS
NEPTUNE

THE FRONTIER OF THE SOLAR SYSTEM

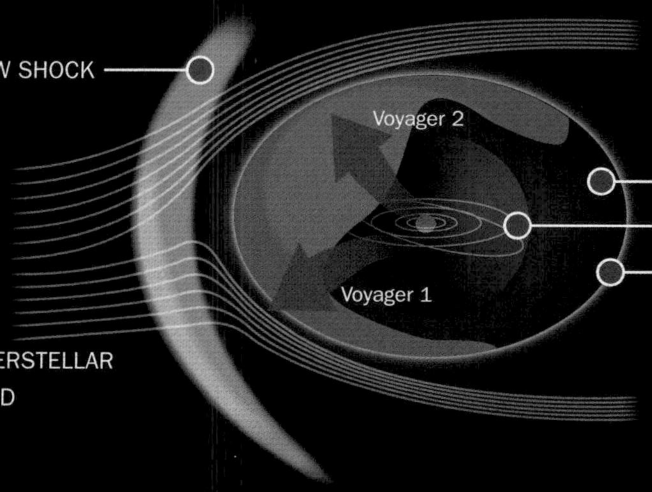

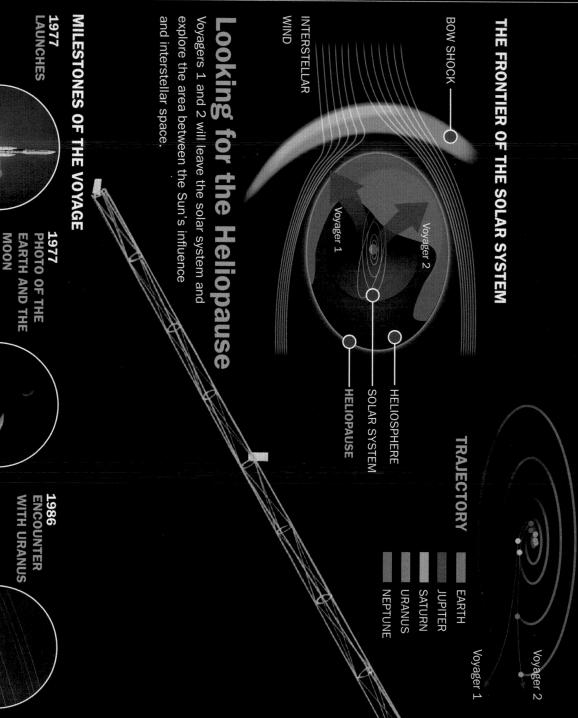

BOW SHOCK
Voyager 2
HELIOSPHERE
SOLAR SYSTEM
HELIOPAUSE
Voyager 1
INTERSTELLAR WIND

Looking for the Heliopause

Voyagers 1 and 2 will leave the solar system and explore the area between the Sun's influence and interstellar space.

MILESTONES OF THE VOYAGE

1977 LAUNCHES

1977 PHOTO OF THE EARTH AND THE MOON

1986 ENCOUNTER WITH URANUS

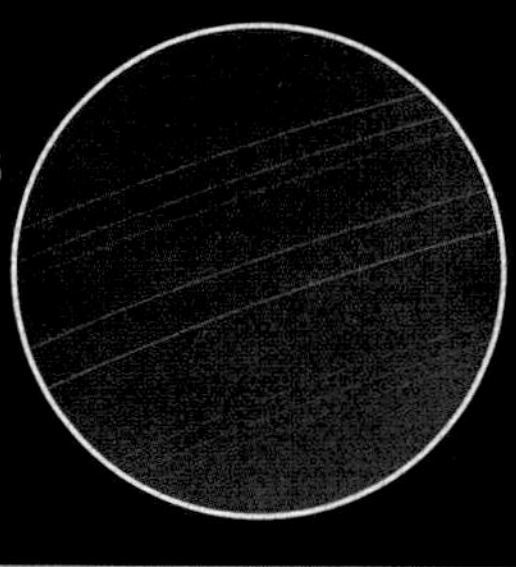

SOLAR SENSOR

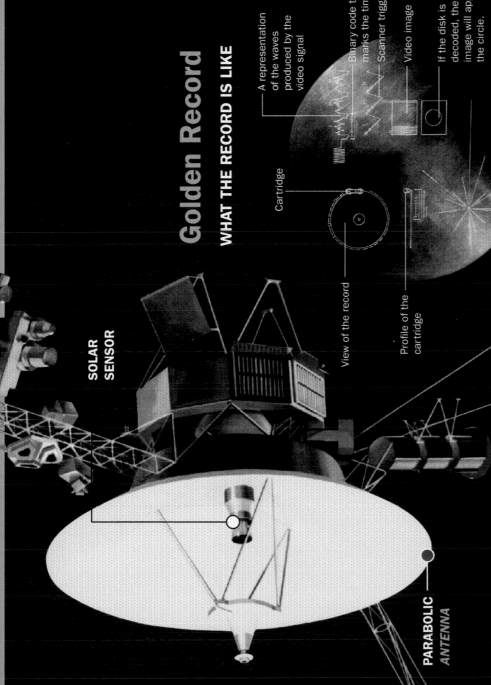

PARABOLIC ***ANTENNA***

Golden Record

WHAT THE RECORD IS LIKE

Cartridge

A representation of the waves produced by the video signal

View of the record

Binary code that marks the time

Scanner trigger

Profile of the cartridge

Video image

If the disk is decoded, the first image will appear in the circle.

This diagram defines the location of our Sun by using 14 directional lines.

Represents the two stages of the hydrogen atom

COMMUNICATION WITH THE EARTH

The antenna must point in the exact direction.

ANTENNA

TECHNICAL SPECIFICATIONS: VOYAGER 1 AND 2

Launch date	**1977**
Useful life	**60 years**
Weight	**1,800 pounds (815 kg)**
Source of energy	**Plutonium**
Organization	**NASA**

11 feet (3.35 m)
11 feet (3.35 m)

1,800 pounds (815 kg)

WEIGHT ON EARTH

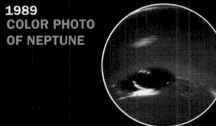

1987
OBSERVATION OF A *SUPERNOVA*

1989
COLOR PHOTO OF NEPTUNE

1998
PASSES PIONEER 10

Pluto: Now a Dwarf

Pluto stopped being the ninth planet of the solar system in 2006 when the International Astronomical Union decided to change the classification of cold, distant Pluto to that of dwarf planet. This tiny body in our solar system has never had an imposing profile, and it has not yet been possible to study it closely. All that is known about Pluto comes through observations made from the Earth or Earth orbit, such as those made by the Hubble Space Telescope. Despite the lack of information gathered about Pluto, it is notable for its unique orbit, the tilt of its axis, and its location within the *Kuiper belt*. All these characteristics make Pluto especially intriguing.

A Double World

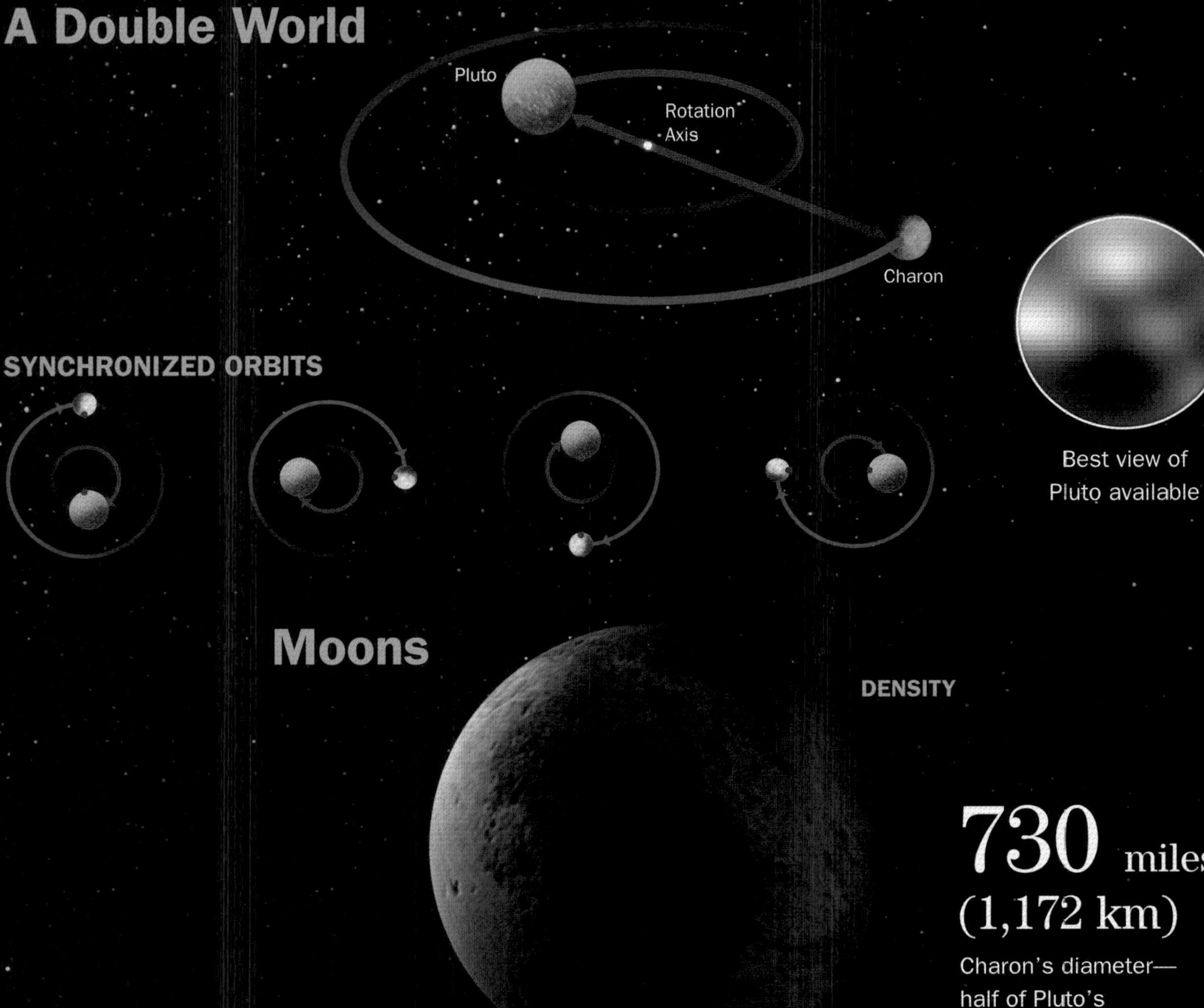
Pluto
Rotation Axis
Charon
SYNCHRONIZED ORBITS

Best view of Pluto available

Moons

DENSITY

730 miles (1,172 km)

Charon's diameter—half of Pluto's

Composition

ATMOSPHERE

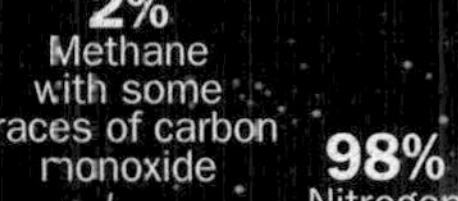
2%
Methane with some traces of carbon monoxide
98%
Nitrogen

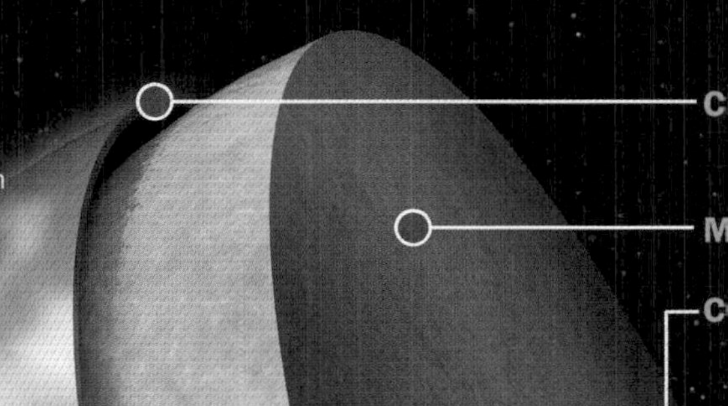
CRUST
MANTLE
CORE
270 miles
(434 km)
570 miles
(920 km)

Surface

CHARACTERISTICS

CONVENTIONAL PLANET SYMBOL 

ESSENTIAL DATA	
Average distance from the Sun	**3,700,000,000 miles (5,900,000,000 km)**
Solar orbit (Plutonian year)	**247.9 years**
Equatorial Diameter	**1,400 miles (2,247 km)**
Orbital speed	**3 miles per second (4.8 km/s)**
*Mass**	**0.002**
*Gravity**	**0.067**
Density	**1.2 ounces per cubic inch (2.05 g/cu cm)**
Average Temperature	**-380° F (-230° C)**
Atmosphere	**Very thin**
Moons	**3**

*In both cases, Earth = 1

AXIS INCLINATION

122°
One rotation lasts 6.387 Earth days.

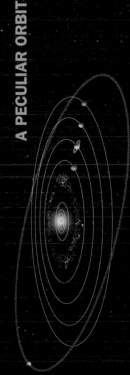

NEW HORIZONS MISSION

A PECULIAR ORBIT

Distant Worlds

Farther even than Neptune, the eighth planet, we find frozen bodies smaller than the Earth's Moon—the more than 100,000 objects forming the *Kuiper belt*, the frozen boundary of our solar system. Recently astronomers of the International Astronomical Union decided to reclassify Pluto as a dwarf planet because of its size and eccentric orbit. Periodic *comets* (comets that appear at regular intervals) originate in the Kuiper belt. Nonperiodic comets, on the other hand, come from the Oort cloud, a gigantic sphere surrounding the entire solar system.

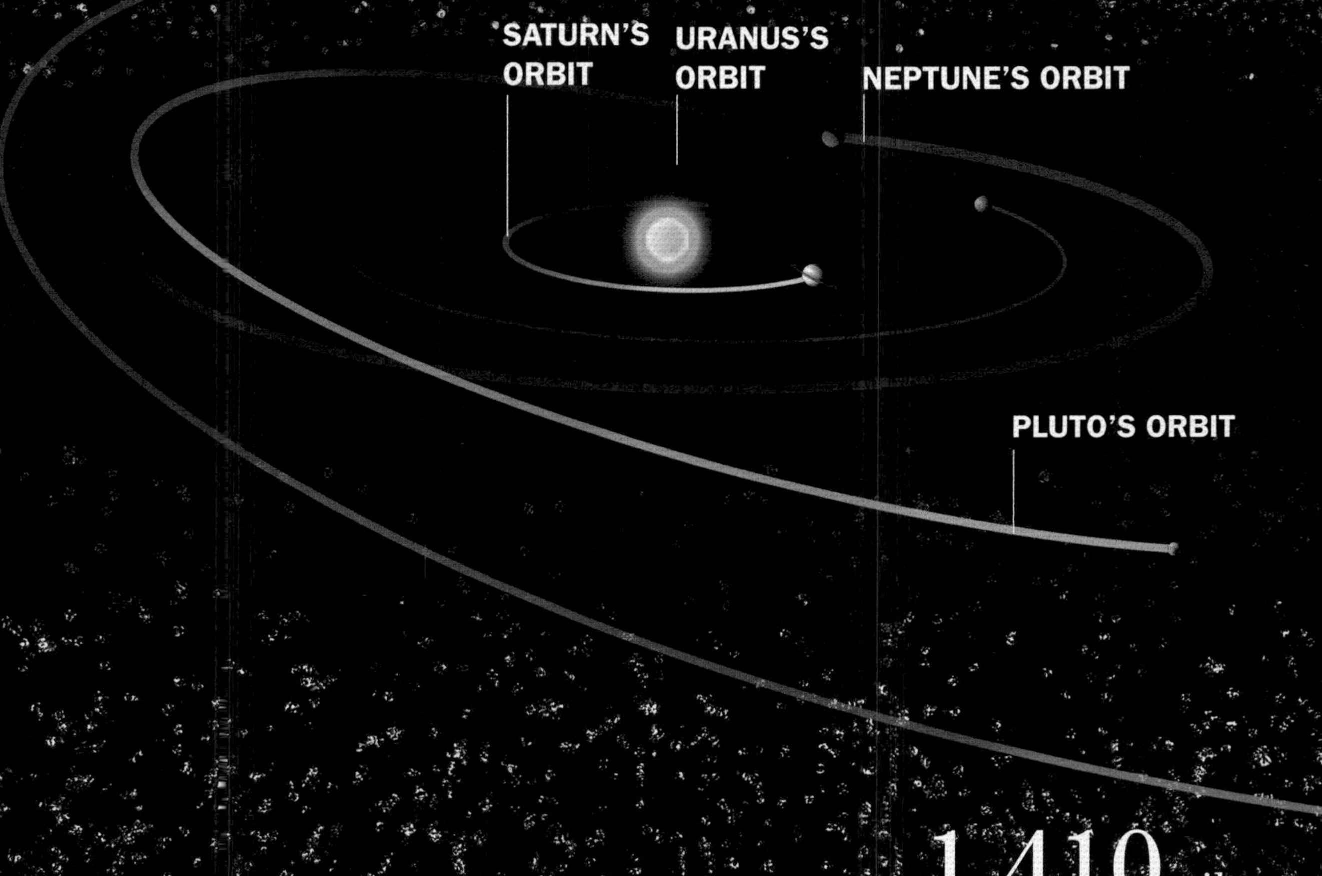
SATURN'S ORBIT
URANUS'S ORBIT
NEPTUNE'S ORBIT
PLUTO'S ORBIT

Kuiper Belt

1,410 miles (2,274 km)

is the diameter of Pluto—750 miles (1,200 km) smaller than the diameter of the Earth's Moon. Because of its size and orbit, Pluto is considered a dwarf planet instead of a planet.

Comparable Sizes

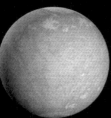

QUAOAR

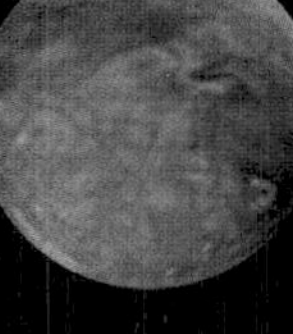

SEDNA

PLUTO

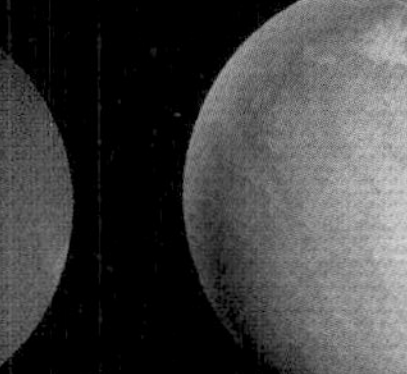

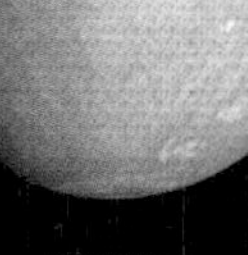

ERIS

200 OR MORE POSSIBLE EXTRA SOLAR PLANETS HAVE BEEN DETECTED

ERIS

ERIS: THE FARTHEST ONE

Extrasolar Planets

For centuries, there has been speculation about the possible existence of planets orbiting other stars in the universe in the same way that the planets of the solar system, including the Earth, revolve around the Sun. Nevertheless, it has been only a little more than a decade since it has been possible to detect such bodies—albeit indirectly—thanks to new *telescopes* and measuring devices with increased sensitivity. The confirmation of the existence of these extrasolar planets suddenly increases the possibility that life might exist in other corners of the cosmos.

Distant Worlds

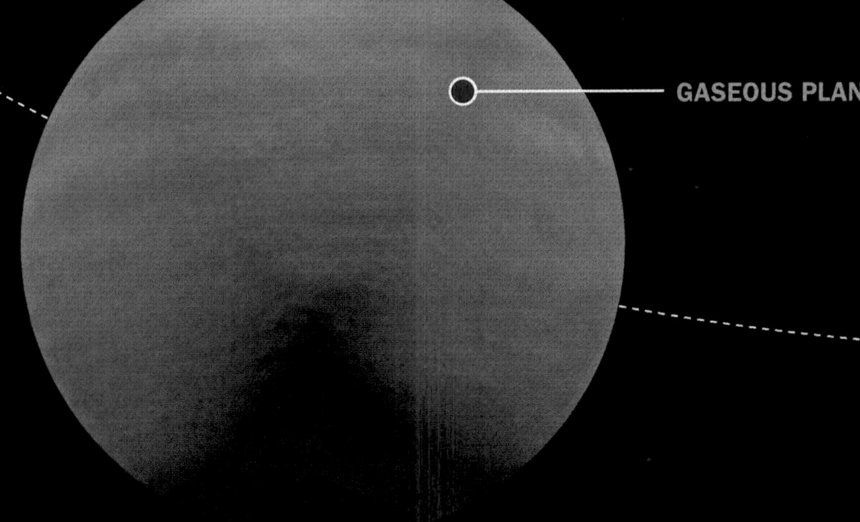
GASEOUS PLANETS

The First Photograph?

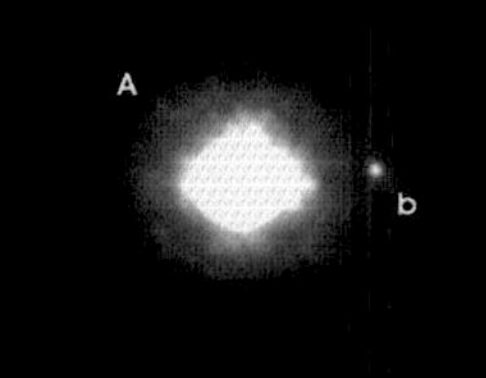
A
b

1.2 days

The time it takes the planet OGLE-TR-56 to orbit its star; it is the shortest orbital period known for a planet.

Notable Extrasolar Planets

Among the extrasolar planets that have been detected, there are surprising differences in their characteristics.

The First
Pegasi 51 b

The Hottest
HD 149026 b

The Most Massive
Undetermined

The Smallest
Gliese 581 c

The Closest
Epsilon Eridani b

The Most Distant
OGLE-2003-BLG-235

STAR

ROCKY PLANETS

A WORLD SIMILAR TO THE EARTH

EARTH

Size: 7,930 miles (12,756 km) in diameter

Mass: 13.17 x 1024 pounds (5.976 x 1024 kg)

Distance from its star: 93 million miles (150 million km), or 1 AU

Temperature: between -112° and 122° F (-80° and 50° C)

Orbital period: 365 days

Water: in gaseous, liquid, and solid states

GLIESE 581 c

Size: 1.5 times the diameter of the Earth

Mass: 4.83 times the Earth's mass

Distance from its star: One 14th the distance of the Earth from the Sun (0.07 AU)

Temperature: unknown, but believed to be between 27° and 104° F (-3° and 40° C)

Orbital period: 13 days

Water: It would have conditions suitable for the existence of liquid water.

12.7 billion years

The age of planet PSR B1620-26b, the oldest of all the known extrasolar planets; this planet orbits a system of binary pulsars. The much younger Earth is "only" about five billion years old.

INDIRECT DETECTION

Star

Planet

Spectrum showing redshift

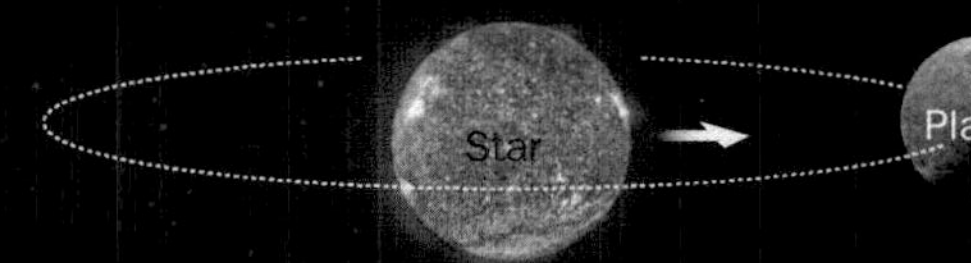

1 REDSHIFT

3 REPEATING CYCLE

Planet

Star

Spectrum showing blueshift

2 BLUESHIFT

Anatomy of Galaxies

Galaxies are rotating groups of stars, gas, and dust. More than 200 years ago, philosopher Immanuel Kant postulated that *nebulae* were island-universes of distant stars. Even though astronomers now know that galaxies are held together by gravitational force, they have not been able to decipher what reasons might be behind galaxies' many shapes. The various types of galaxies range from ovals of old stars to spirals with arms of young stars and bright gases. The center of a galaxy has the greatest accumulation of stars. The *Milky Way Galaxy* is now known to be so big that rays of light, which travel at 186,000 miles (300,000 km) per second, take 100,000 years to cross from one end to the other.

Star Cities

The Sombrero Galaxy

COLLISION

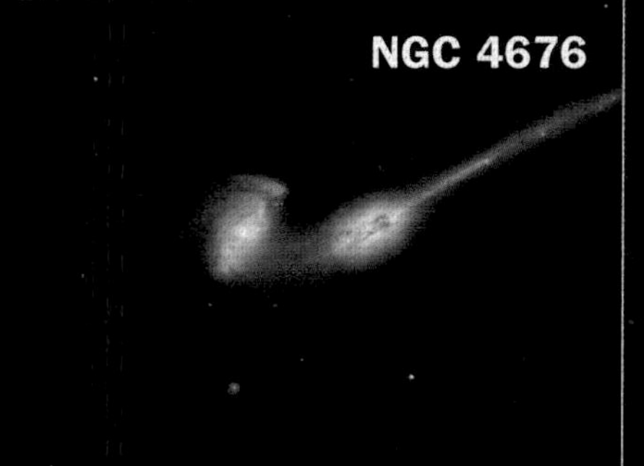

NGC 4676

1 1.2 BILLION YEARS AGO

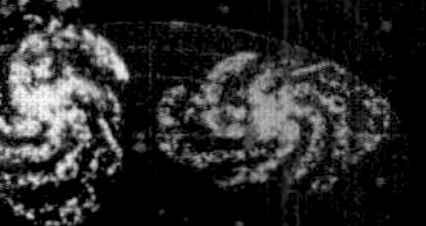

2 300 MILLION YEARS LATER

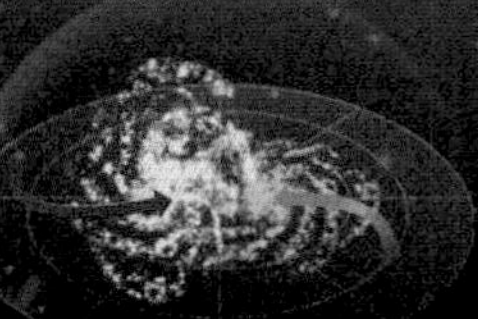

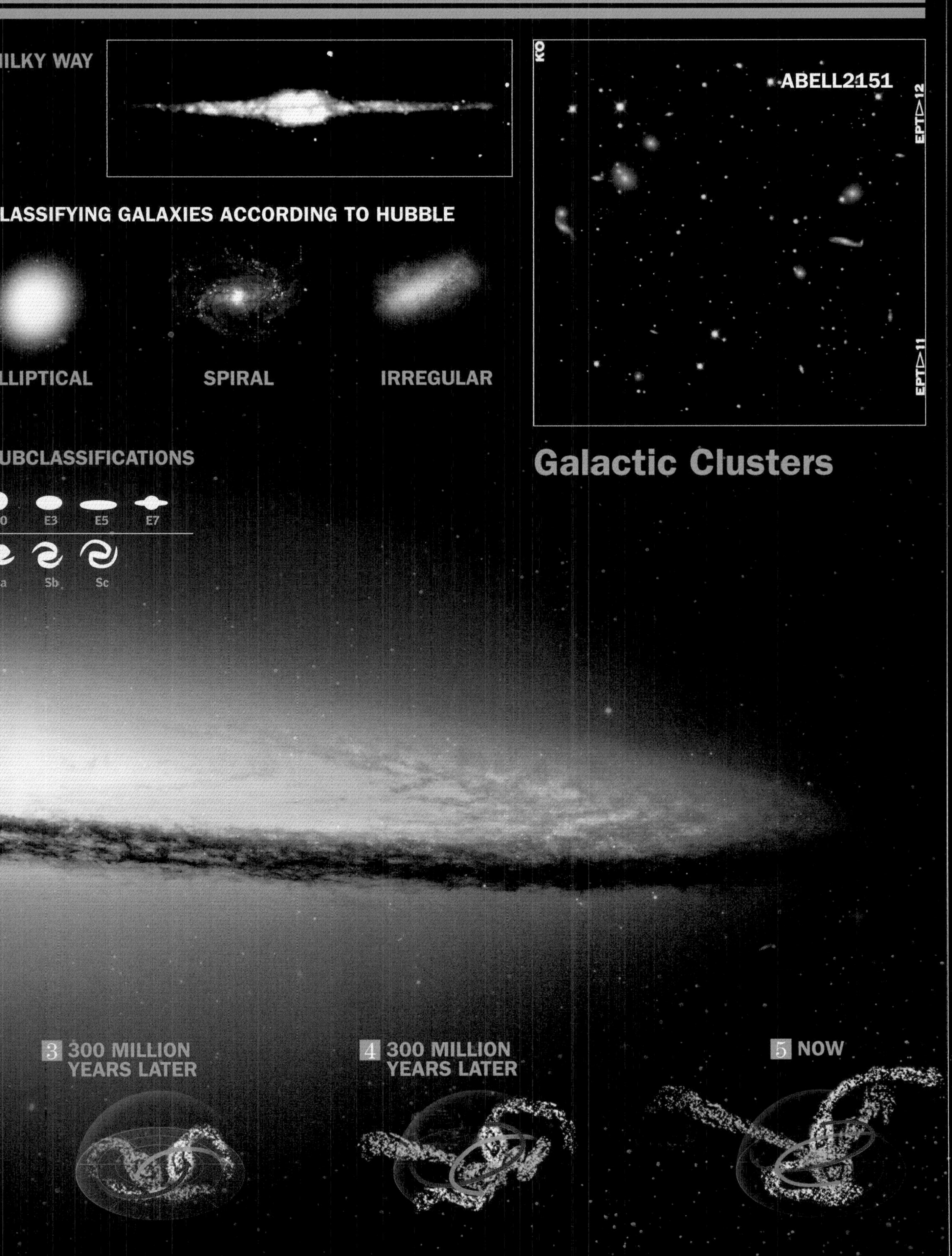
MILKY WAY
CLASSIFYING GALAXIES ACCORDING TO HUBBLE
ELLIPTICAL
SPIRAL
IRREGULAR
SUBCLASSIFICATIONS
E0
E3
E5
E7
Sa
Sb
Sc
KO
ABELL2151
EPT▷12
EPT▷11
Galactic Clusters
3 300 MILLION YEARS LATER
4 300 MILLION YEARS LATER
5 NOW

Stellar Metropolis

For a long time, our galaxy (called the Milky Way because of its resemblance to a stream of milk in the night sky) was a true enigma. It was Galileo Galilei who, in 1610, first pointed a *telescope* at the Milky Way and saw that the weak whitish strip was composed of thousands and thousands of stars that appeared to almost touch each other. Little by little, astronomers began to realize that all these stars, like our own Sun, were part of the enormous ensemble—the galaxy that is our stellar metropolis.

Large Magellanic Cloud
MILKY WAY
Small Magellanic Cloud
Andromeda Galaxy
Triangle Galaxy

Structure of the Milky Way

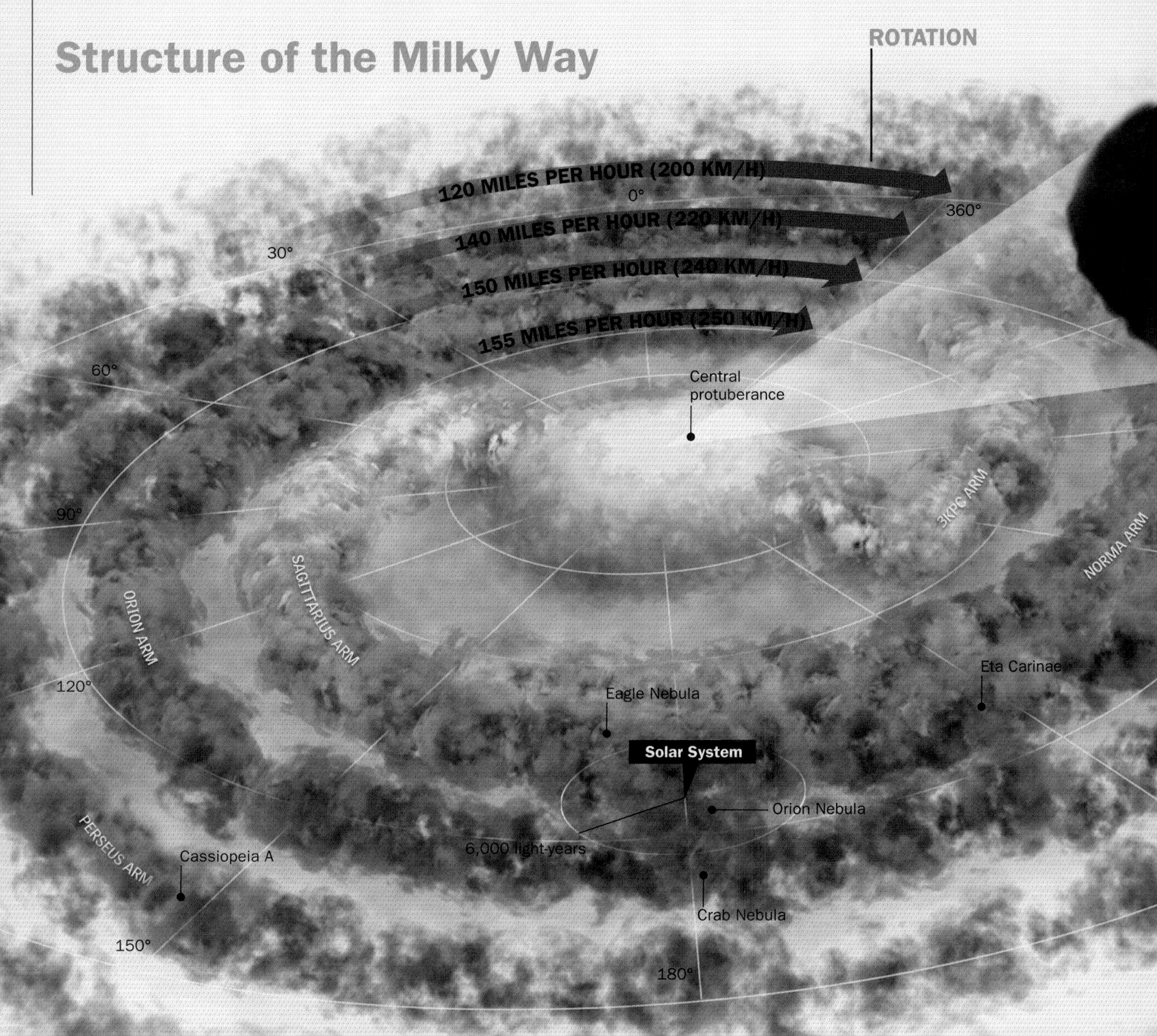
ROTATION
120 MILES PER HOUR (200 KM/H)
140 MILES PER HOUR (220 KM/H)
150 MILES PER HOUR (240 KM/H)
155 MILES PER HOUR (250 KM/H)
0°
360°
30°
60°
90°
120°
150°
180°
Central protuberance
3KPC ARM
NORMA ARM
SAGITTARIUS ARM
ORION ARM
PERSEUS ARM
Eta Carinae
Eagle Nebula
Solar System
Orion Nebula
6,000 light-years
Cassiopeia A
Crab Nebula

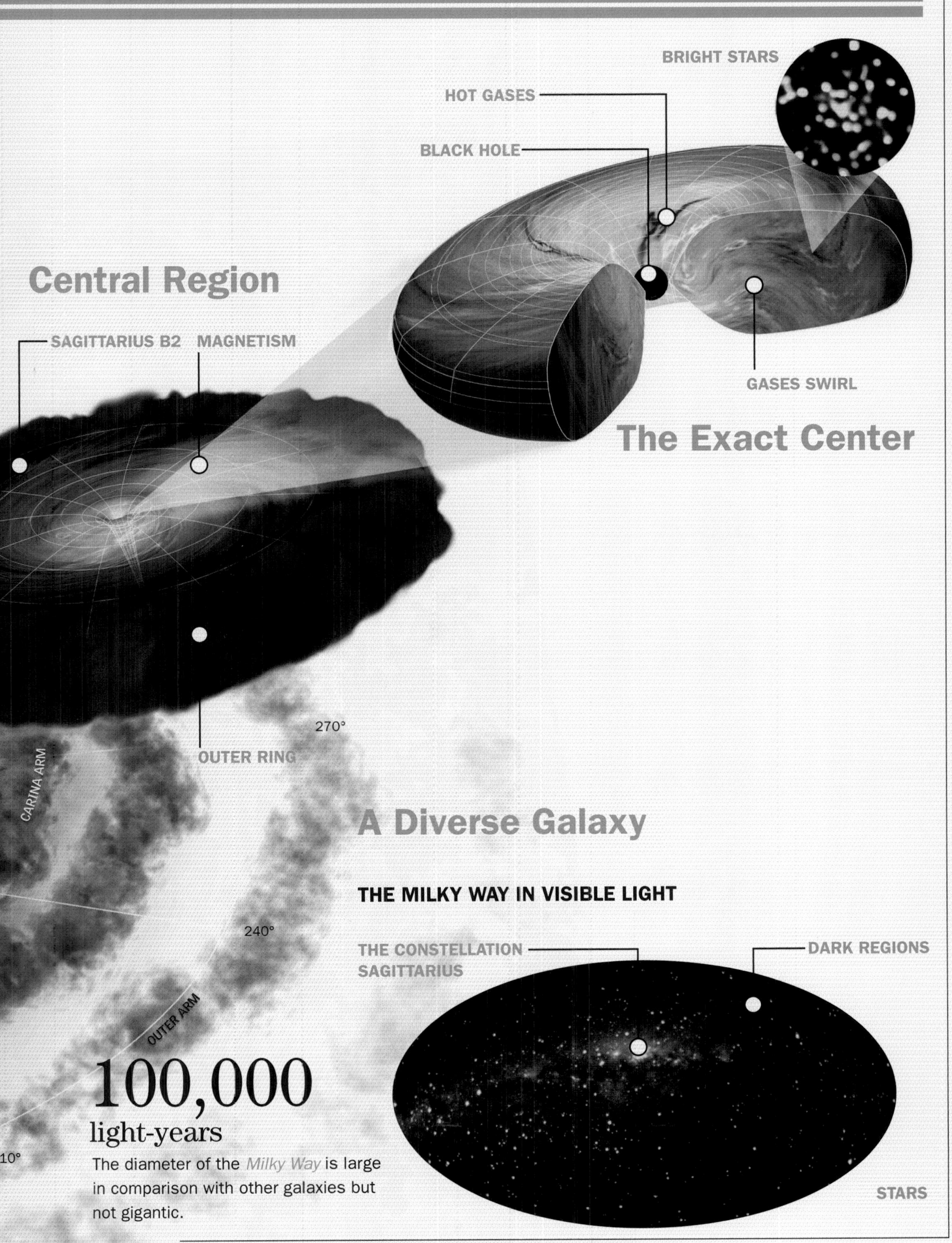
BRIGHT STARS
HOT GASES
BLACK HOLE
GASES SWIRL
SAGITTARIUS B2
MAGNETISM
OUTER RING
270°
CARINA ARM
240°
OUTER ARM
210°
THE CONSTELLATION SAGITTARIUS
DARK REGIONS
STARS

Central Region

The Exact Center

A Diverse Galaxy

THE MILKY WAY IN VISIBLE LIGHT

100,000
light-years

The diameter of the *Milky Way* is large in comparison with other galaxies but not gigantic.

Stellar Evolution

Stars are born in *nebulae*, which are giant clouds of gas (mainly *hydrogen*) and dust that float in space. Stars can have a life span of millions, or even billions, of years. The biggest stars have the shortest lives, because they consume their nuclear fuel (hydrogen) at a very accelerated rate. Other stars, like the Sun, burn fuel at a slower rate and may live some 10 billion years. Many times, a star's size indicates its age. Smaller stars are the youngest, and bigger stars are approaching their end, either through cooling or by exploding as a *supernova*.

Massive Star

More than 8 solar masses

1 PROTOSTAR

2 STAR

Small Star

Less than 8 solar masses

Life Cycle of a Star

1 PROTOSTAR

2 STAR

3 RED SUPERGIANT

4 SUPERNOVA

5 BLACK HOLE

5 NEUTRON STAR

6 BLACK DWARF

3 RED GIANT

5 WHITE DWARF

4 PLANETARY NEBULA

95% of stars
end their lives as white dwarfs. Other (larger) stars explode as supernovae, illuminating galaxies for weeks, although their brightness is often obscured by the gases and dust.

Sprinkled With Stars

Chi1
Orionis
Xi
Orionis
Mu
Orionis
Betelgeuse

Constellations are groups of stars thought to represent different animals, mythological characters, and other figures. Constellations were invented by ancient civilizations to serve as reference points in the Earth's sky. There are 88 of these collections of stars. Although each star in a constellation appears related to the others, it is actually very far from them. Not all the constellations are visible at the same time from any one place on the Earth.

ORIGIN

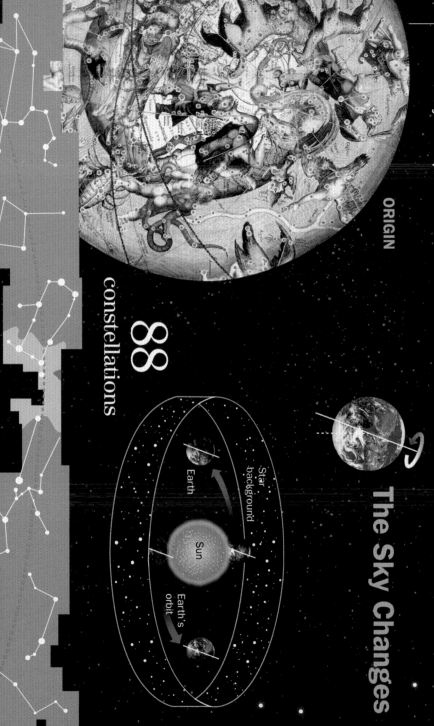

The Sky Changes

Star
background
Earth
Sun
Earth's
orbit
88
constellations
LEO
CANCER
GEMINI
TAURUS
ARIES
PISCES

The Constellations of the Zodiac

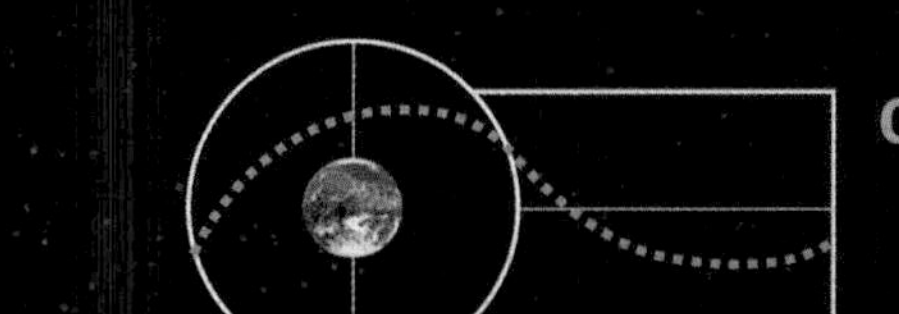

OBSERVING THE CONSTELLATIONS

Different Cultures

Omicron Orionis
Heka
Pi2 Orionis
Bellatrix
Pi3 Orionis
Pi4 Orionis
Pi5 Orionis
Pi6 Orionis
Mintaka
Alnilam
Alnitak
Rigel
Saiph

THE MYSTERY OF GIZA

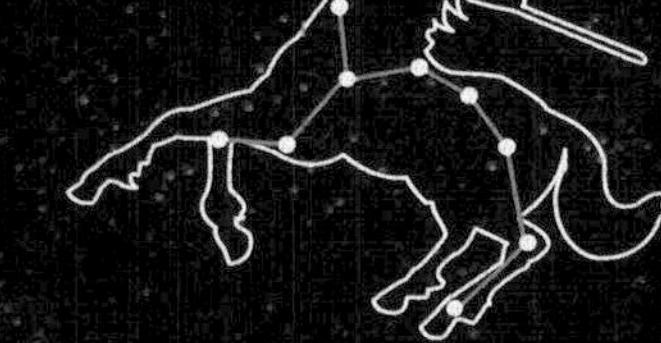

SCORPIUS

URSA MAJOR

THE CENTAUR

Babylon

The Babylonians conceived of the zodiac 2,000 years ago as a way of measuring time, using it as a symbolic calendar.

13

OPHIUCHUS
LIBRA
SAGITTARIUS
AQUARIUS
CAPRICORN
VIRGO
SCORPIUS

Construction Debris: Asteroids and Meteorites

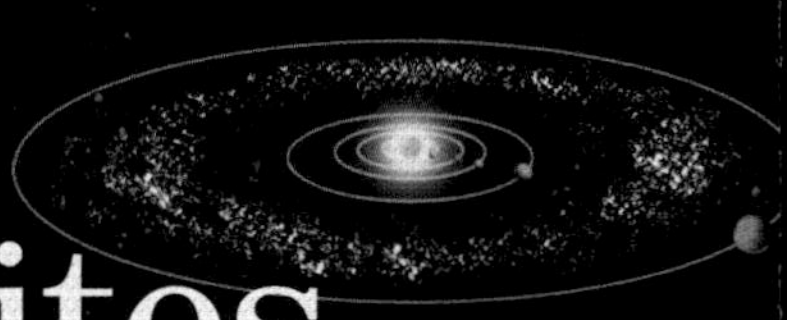

Ever since the formation of the solar system, the melting, collision, and rupture of various materials played an essential role in the formation of the planets. Remnants of this process remain in the form of rock debris, which serves as witness to the formation of the solar system. These objects are also associated with episodes that influenced subsequent evolutionary processes on Earth. They are a possible cause of the mass extinction of dinosaurs more than 60 million years ago.

Extraterrestrial

While some meteorites are from the Moon or Mars, most are associated with asteroids.

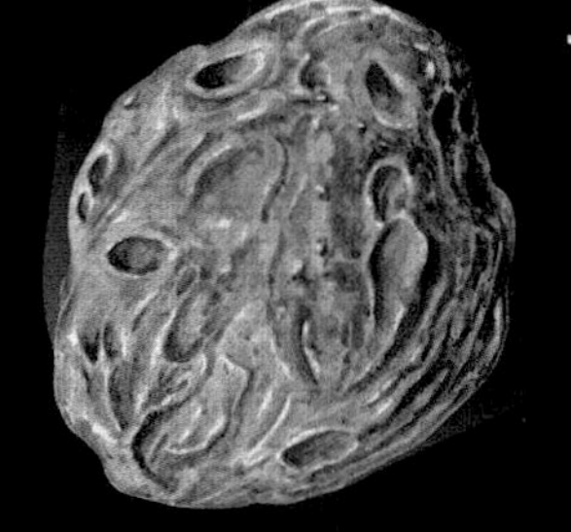

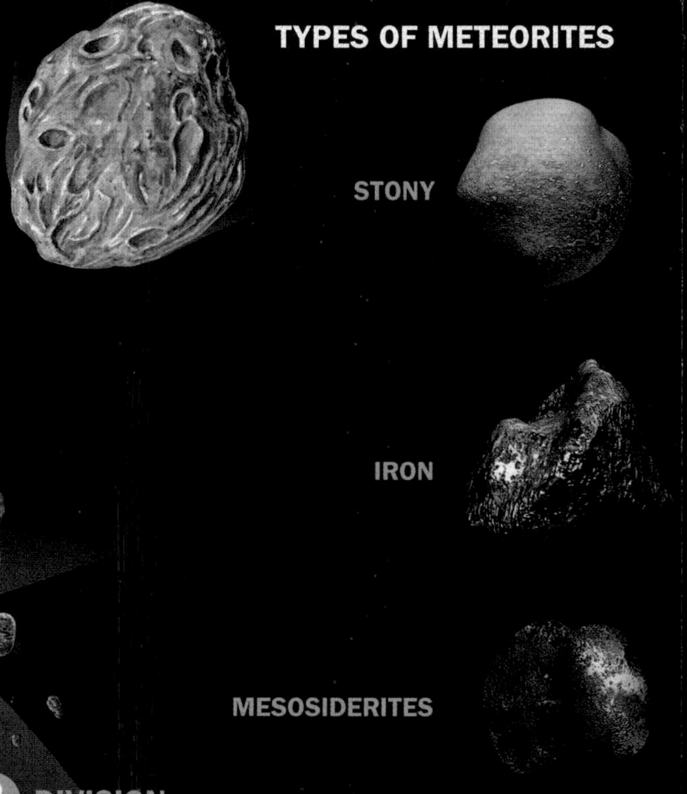

TYPES OF METEORITES

STONY

IRON

MESOSIDERITES

A HUGE METEORITE STRIKES

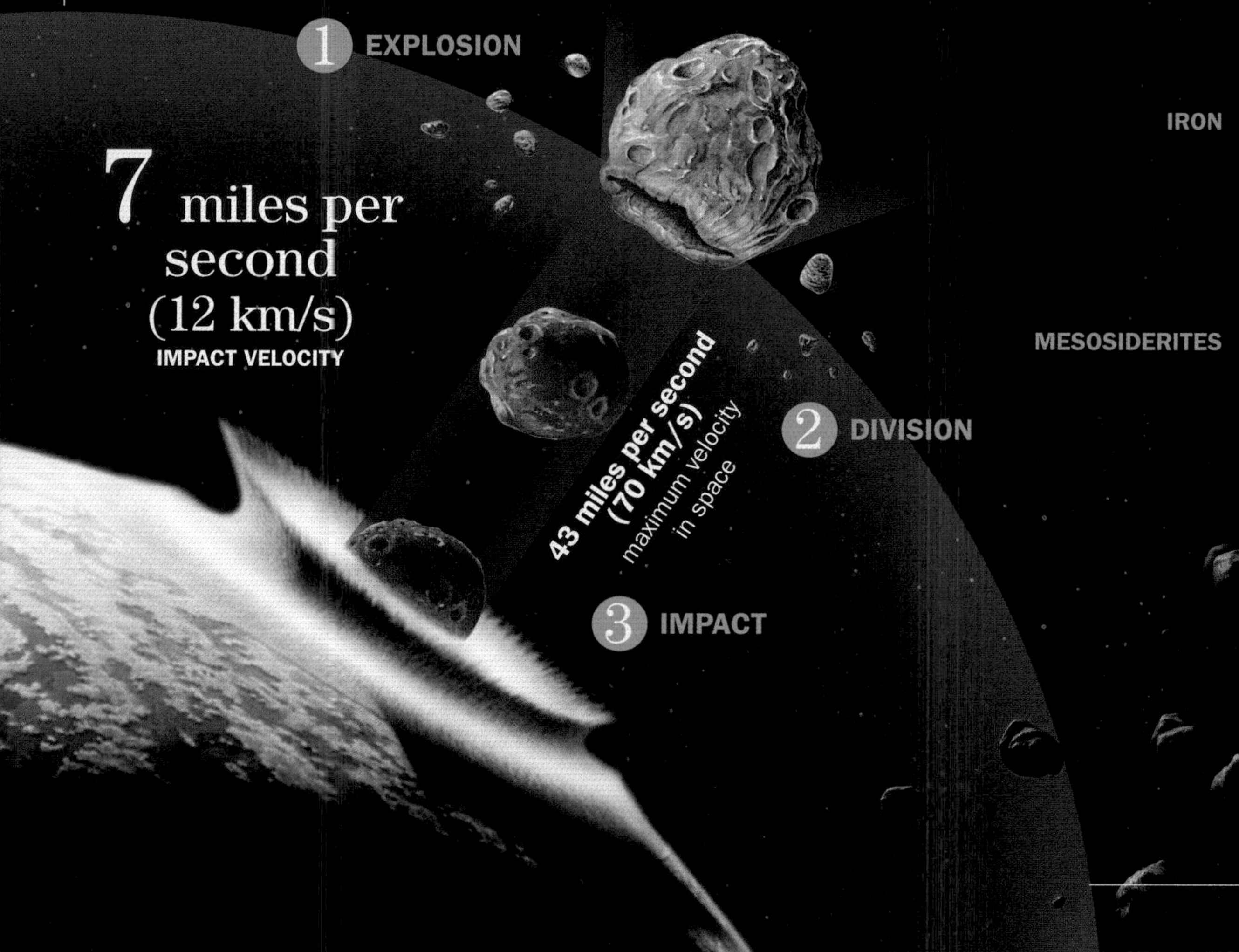

1 EXPLOSION

2 DIVISION

3 IMPACT

7 miles per second (12 km/s)
IMPACT VELOCITY

43 miles per second (70 km/s)
maximum velocity in space

Asteroids

HIDALGO completes a solar orbit every 14 Earth years.

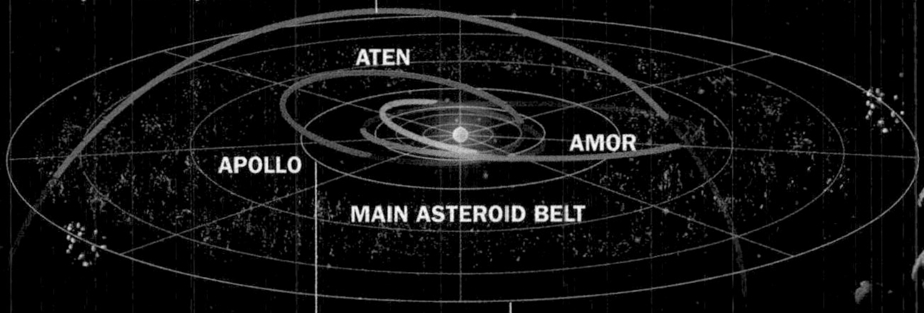

ATEN

AMOR

APOLLO

MAIN ASTEROID BELT

Mars's orbit

Jupiter's orbit

The Trojans trace an orbit similar to Jupiter's, one group in front of the planet and another behind it.

IDA

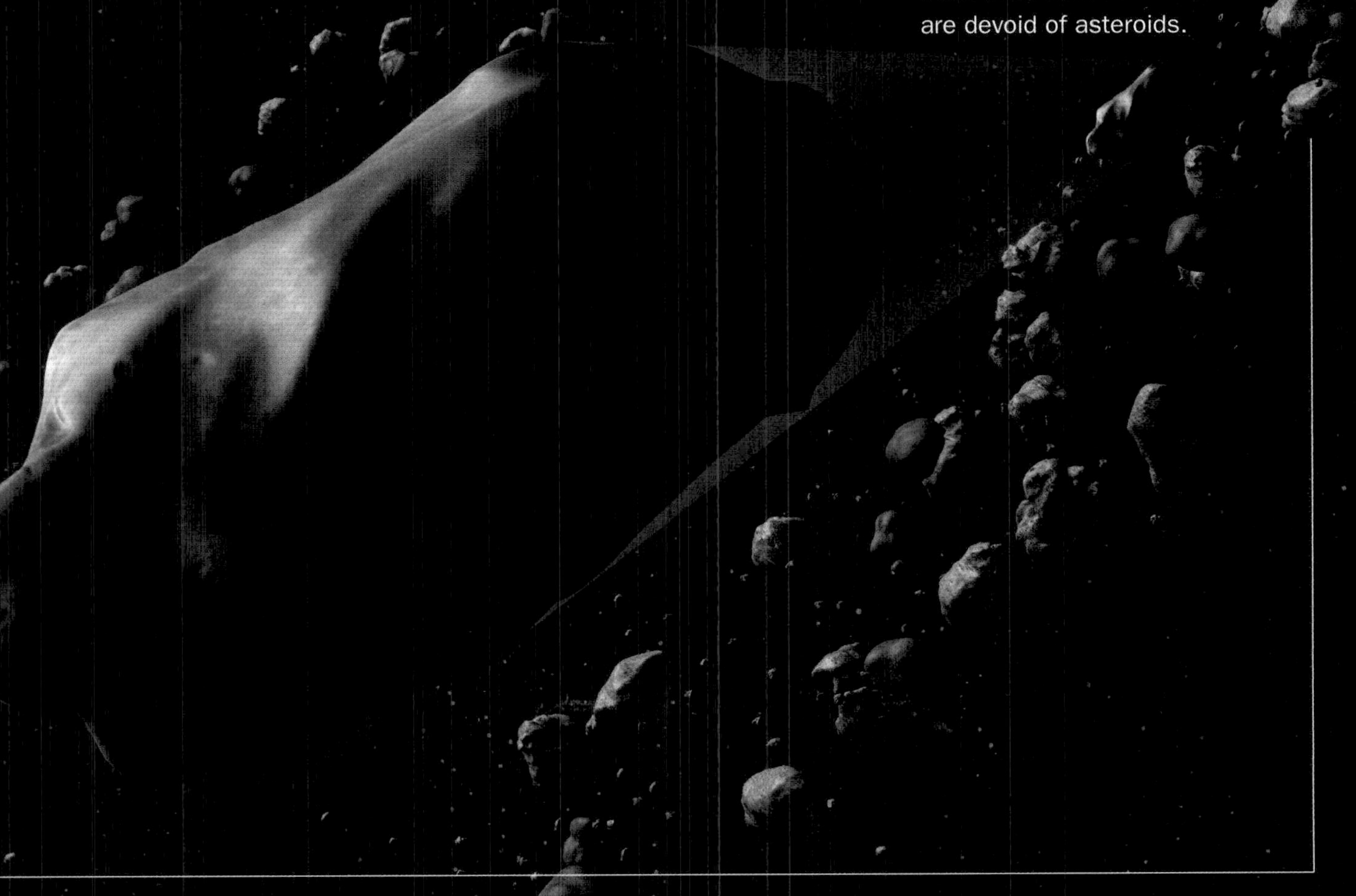

15%

The percentage of the total mass of the asteroids compared to the mass of the Moon

Tighten Your Belt

The asteroid belt contains millions of asteroids.

KIRKWOOD

The Kirkwood gaps are the open areas in the main asteroid belt that are devoid of asteroids.

Those with a Tail

Comets are small, deformed objects a few miles in diameter that are normally frozen and dark. Made of dust, rock, gases, and organic molecules rich in carbon, comets are usually found in orbits beyond that of Neptune in the *Kuiper belt* or in the Oort cloud. Occasionally a comet, such as Halley's comet, veers toward the interior of the solar system, where its ice is heated and sublimates, forming a head and long, spectacular tails of gases and dust.

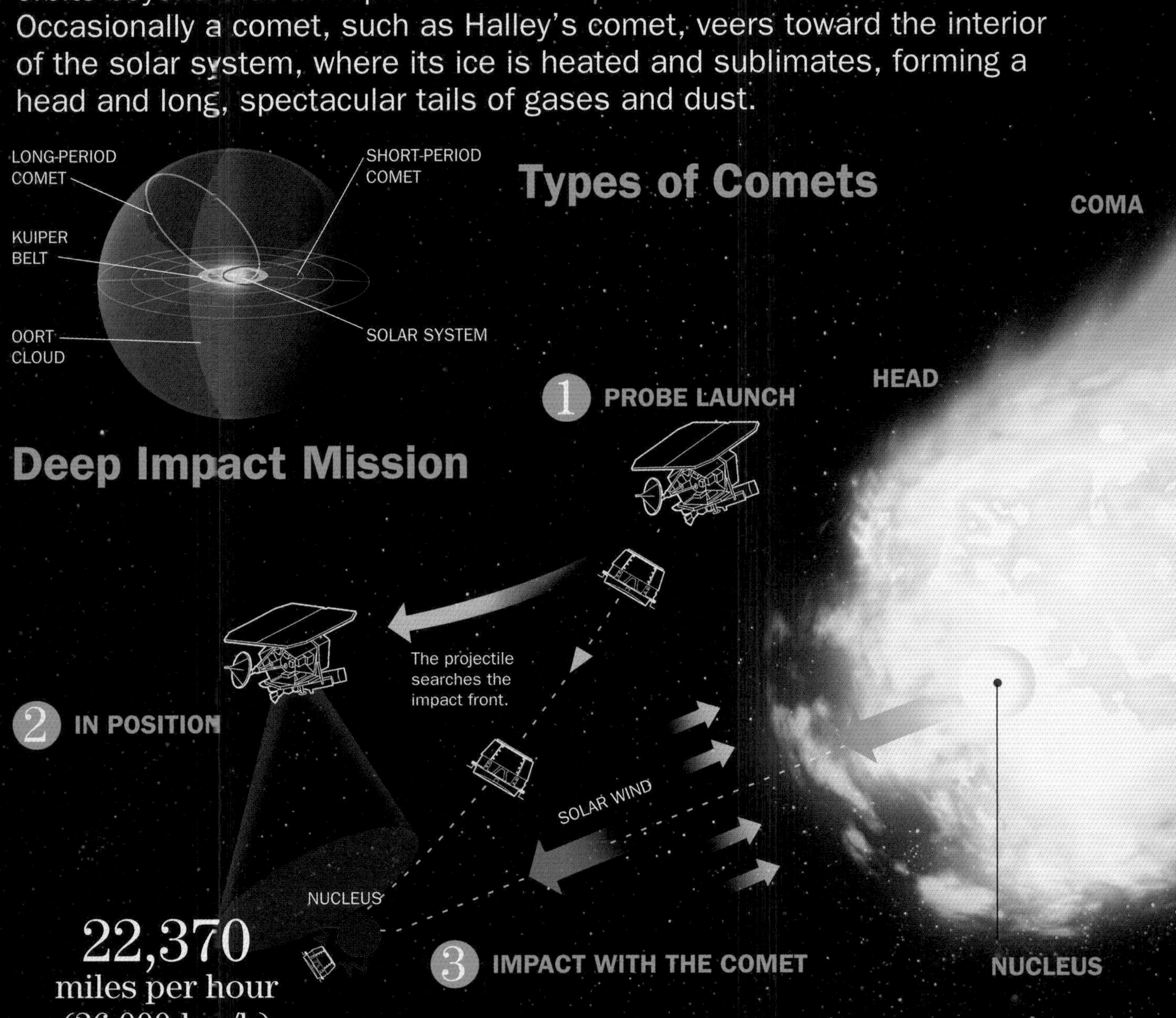
LONG-PERIOD COMET
SHORT-PERIOD COMET
KUIPER BELT
SOLAR SYSTEM
OORT CLOUD
COMA
HEAD
NUCLEUS
1 PROBE LAUNCH
The projectile searches the impact front.
2 IN POSITION
SOLAR WIND
NUCLEUS
3 IMPACT WITH THE COMET

Types of Comets

Deep Impact Mission

22,370 miles per hour (36,000 km/h)

VELOCITY OF THE COMET IMPACT

PREVIOUS MISSIONS

GIOTTO

DEEP SPACE

STARDUST

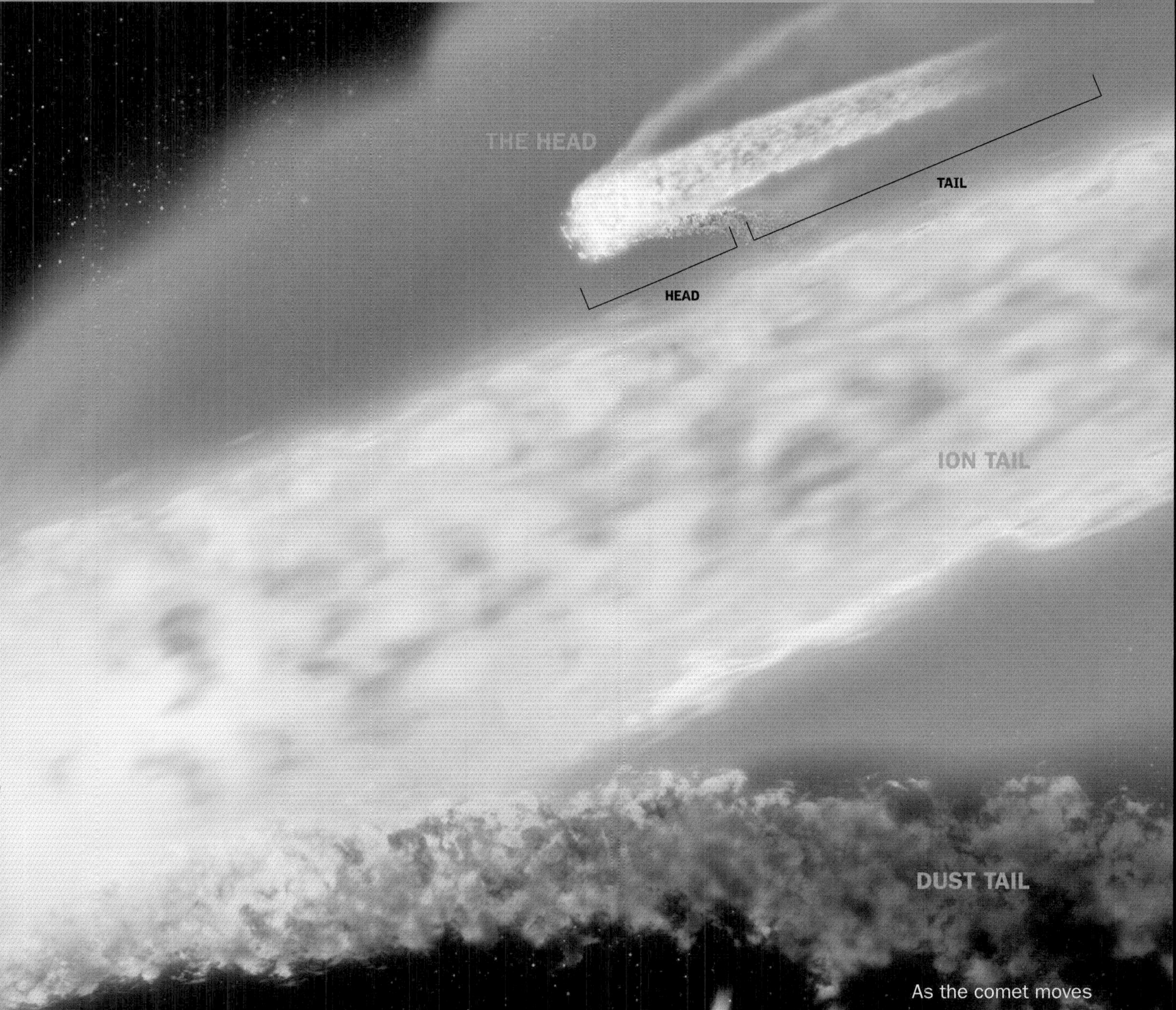

THE HEAD

TAIL

HEAD

ION TAIL

DUST TAIL

FORMATION OF THE TAIL AND HEAD

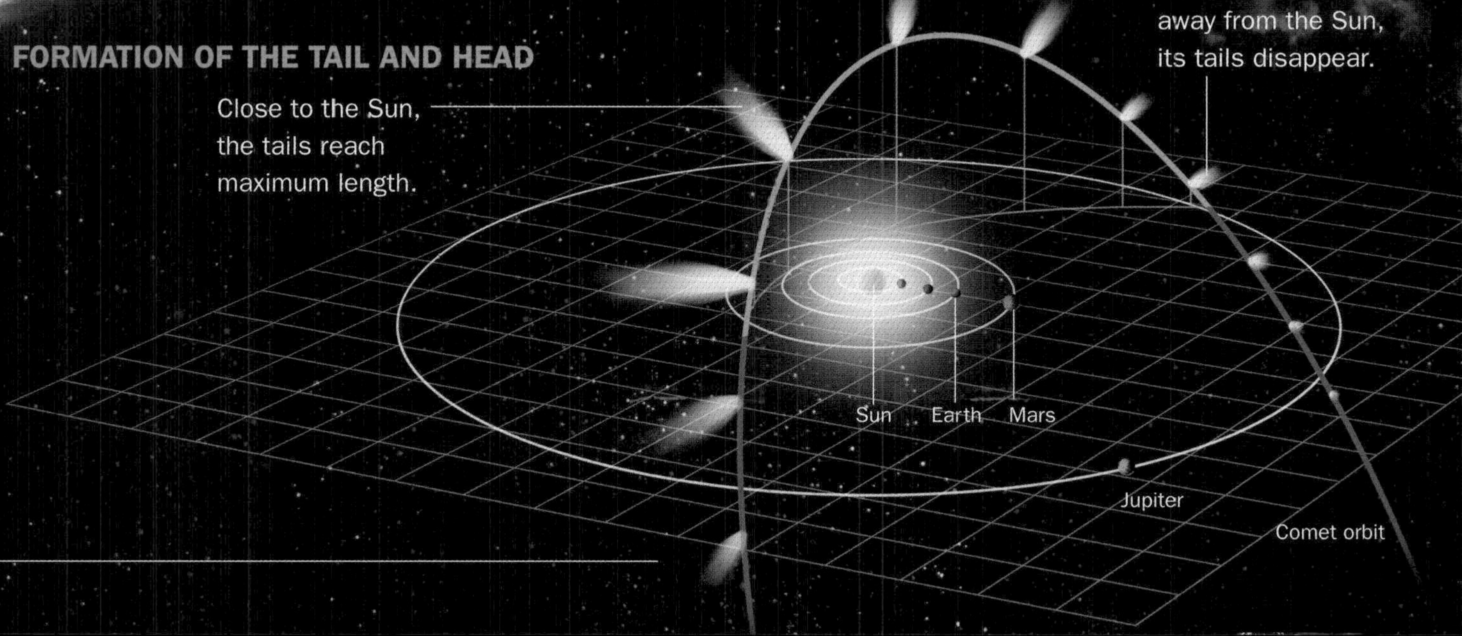

Close to the Sun, the tails reach maximum length.

As the comet moves away from the Sun, its tails disappear.

Sun

Earth

Mars

Jupiter

Comet orbit

Seeing Stars

Thanks to current technology, we can enjoy the displays of light and shadow that make up the objects of our universe. Although not all of these objects are known, it can be said without a doubt that most of the atoms that make up our bodies have been born in the interior of stars.

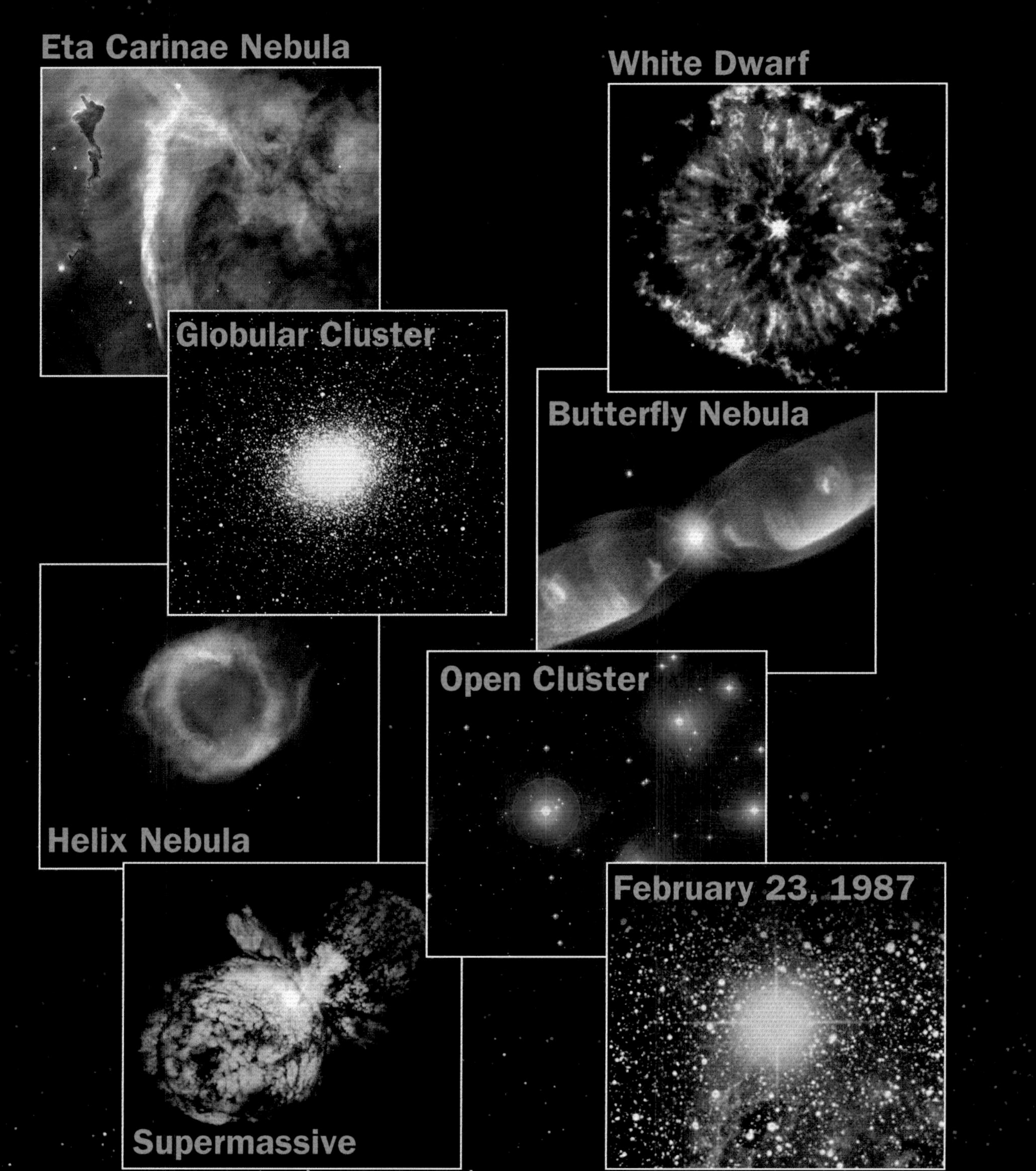
Eta Carinae Nebula
White Dwarf
Globular Cluster
Butterfly Nebula
Open Cluster
Helix Nebula
February 23, 1987
Supermassive